W9-DBK-126

OUT AROUND CAROLYN

A Community Remembers Summers Past

For David — my memories
you go back to a wonderful
fall term at Macalester over
30 years ago — here are
some of my even earlier
memories. Bill Donovan

OUT AROUND CAROLYN

A Community
Remembers
Summers Past

William P. Donovan, EDITOR
Peter McDonald, ART

© 2002 W.P.Donovan

All rights reserved. No part of this book may be reproduced in any form without permission from the editors.

ISBN 0-9721458-0-X

Cover:
Looking towards Carolyn from Eagle Island.
Photo by W.P. Donovan

Back cover:
Top, photo by K.P. Donovan
Left bottom, photo by P.A.Donovan

CONTENTS

FOREWORD AND DEDICATION

There are thousands of rocky islands along the eastern shore of Georgian Bay, the large body of water extending into Ontario from Lake Huron. On many of them vacationers built summer cottages, some as early as 1900. Those islands lying between Parry Sound to the south and Pointe au Baril to the north form one important group, out of many. This is the story of seventeen islands belonging to this group and of those who spent their summers there. That story has been preserved in the memories of the islanders and passed by word of mouth from one generation to another and from those already a part of this community to those who joined it through marriage, friendship, or purchase. Why then record these stories now in this book? The reasons for a change from an aural-oral tradition to a written one are somewhat mysterious and always, I suspect, somewhat similar. It is easier to note those factors which led to the start of this endeavor. The two who initiated the project, Pete McDonald and Bill Donovan, grew up together here and share an interest in, and a love of, the many stories they heard first as children.

As we grow older and memories begin to fade and as so many of the original summer inhabitants are no longer alive to tell their own stories, much of this lore will soon be lost, if not collected in a systematic way. Finally, the appearance of Ruth Hall McCuaig's history of the larger community of Pointe au Baril served as an inspiration and a model. Its limited treatment of our small group of islanders invited this supplement. Work on this history began in earnest in 1986.

Pete and I decided at the outset that this history would be a collaborative effort in which everyone would be invited to contribute accounts and favorite anecdotes. Pete would provide appropriate graphics and sketches and I a general introduction, explanatory notes to the individual contributions where needed and a catalogue or gazeteer of the islands covered. We invited submissions of photographs or other memorabilia for possible inclusion. Unfortunately too many of those first islanders had died before we began to collect material so their contributions come second hand, for the most part, or from letters written late in life, or sometimes from things written much earlier that were passed down. From later generations we have been blessed with many accounts. In order to preserve chronological continuity I have not simply reprinted these contributions as submitted, but have taken the liberty of making selections and arranging them to form a more continuous narrative from the beginning down almost to the present.

The ancient Greek historian Thucydides commented upon the unreliability of human memory, a theme frequently echoed by contributors and editors to this work. Since I share his concern with accuracy, I have tried to verify, where possible, all names and dates, but discrepancies persist and errors remain. Written records, where they exist, have been consulted to corroborate, correct, or supply information. These include the official land registrations, the list of islands for sale in the district of Parry Sound published by the Department of Lands and Forests in 1926, the diaries of Carrie Bartow which she kept for most summers between 1915 and 1978, the notebooks and photograph albums of Leonard Giovannoli covering especially the period from the end of World War I to the outbreak of World War II, and the letters of Gladys Dickey and of Dorothy Dickey Donovan to W.P. Donovan from 1952 to 1968.

Our story begins with a brief reconstruction of our common history and of the features of cottage life we have shared over many summers spent here on our islands. Then follow the essays, memoirs, and anecdotes arranged in roughly chronological order. Finally there is the gazeteer listing each inhabited island in the area covered by this history together with the chronology of owners and cottages.

This is not a record of major events and great deeds like those which cried out for writers of the great histories of the past to compose their records for posterity. These are stories of those who would appear to most as ordinary people who describe rather ordinary, if extraordinarily pleasant, summers. These islanders do form, however, an identifiable group and reflection on our summers here produces accounts which demonstrate that we do share a similar lore about ourselves. Those who have joined our number as adults over the years, usually through marriage, sometimes through purchase, have come to know the experience of suddenly encountering what must seem a very closed society whose members, whenever gathered, begin to rehearse the many anecdotes which constitute its lore, a lore which in turn helps to constitute and define the community. As an archaeologist and historian I am struck by how similar, albeit on a modest scale, we are to other societies I have studied. In all there is a shared mythology, a series of stories, told generation after generation which presents a picture of the past. This picture, however inaccurate it may be, especially in details, provides a people with a vision of its own past, defines its values, and sets it apart as an identifiable society, be it a summer colony, a village, a tribe, or a nation. Experience suggests that these mythologies are written down whenever change from whatever cause threatens to produce major transformations in the group. The written history is, therefore, not so much an effort to record the past as an effort to preserve a society and its way of life as it faces an uncertain future. This history is no exception and this understanding provides the framework for the introductory essay. I leave it to the readers to judge, on the basis of the contributions from participants in this enterprise, whether or not this analysis is justified.

Why should our group of islanders face now an uncertain future? My answer to this question presupposes that there has been, and is, an unstated ethos which has been formed among us. Simply stated it is that these islands constitute a part of the wilderness, not a "lakeland, playland," to quote the slogan of our Parry Sound radio station, not a summer resort. For us our primary communion here each summer is with nature, not fellow vacationing human beings. It is not that we do not socialize with each other, but that we do not share the major emphasis upon such social interaction of other resort areas, nor their characteristic forms, the parties, night life, nor the athletic activities like golf and tennis all of which are found in urban as well as in vacation communities. The stress on wilderness, nature, and being set apart from the "summer resort" are, therefore, essential features, and always have been, of our islanders and have caused us to see ourselves as, not better, but different. But today the greater demands on vacation land, the increased value of island property, improved boats and channels, improved highways, helicopters and airplanes, the ever growing population of Toronto, all threaten our way of life here. On a typical holiday weekend it is hard to convince oneself any longer that we are in a wilderness area and not at a summer resort. And what of the years ahead?

Pete and I have collected these stories, then, at the very least, in the hope that what has been important to us will not be lost and, if the worst comes to pass and our way of life cannot be preserved, at least it can be remembered. We hope that young people will come to recognize and to value those aspects of Georgian Bay and its islands which so attracted our earliest summer settlers. We have compiled this history to commemorate those very settlers for the values which they passed on as a heritage to succeeding generations. Every history has its heroes, heroes who, to those who come after, like events, appear almost legendary. And our community is no exception. We have our own heroes about whom stories are told and whose memories are ever kept alive, whose lives and deeds somehow reveal the essential qualities and values of us all. As I have collected, edited, and thought about all that has been submitted for this history, three figures, among many, seem especially to match the description of a defining hero. Stories are told about all three, all three are especially associated in our minds with a great interest in nature, in the flora and fauna of these islands and waters, and there is an almost legendary quality about them as well. Finally, all three have left, in writing, a record of their interest in, and love of nature: Gladys Dickey in an illustrated book for children on the wildlife of the islands, Dix McDonald in his notebooks and specimens of botanical life, and Leonard Giovannoli in his notebooks and pictures of zoological life. The interests of all three stimulated and focused those of all who knew them and characterize what the rest of us have come to think of as defining our small community. This history is dedicated to their memory and to their example.

Gladys Dickey
1888-1984

Leonard Giovannoli
1901-1994

Dix McDonald
1920-1946

ACKNOWLEDGMENTS

Before I began to thank those who helped transform the idea of a written history into its realization, I want to thank those who made our summers on these islands possible. Without our neighbors, the year-round residents of Pointe au Baril, we would not have this story to tell. They built and maintained our cottages. They ferried us to and from our islands. They provided all the services essential to our life here. They are part of our story and we are grateful for the summers they have given us.

The writing of this history has been a collaborative project. First, I am indebted to the many in our community who wrote for inclusion. The contributing authors are MARY ELLEN BAKER, DUDLEY CURRY, BILL DONOVAN, BOB DONOVAN, KEVIN DONOVAN, SARAH DONOVAN, GEORGE ERDMANN, MOLLY FRANKLIN, GARY FRENCH, LEONARD GIOVANNOLI, HELEN GROVE, JEAN HOFMANN, WENDY HOFMANN, TOM McCONNELL, PETE McDONALD, ERNIE POPE, JOHN WATSON, BABS WILSON.

Two others, CARRIE BARTOW and GLADYS DICKEY, who died before we started this project, left written material that I have used to enrich these pages.

I have also enjoyed the contributions of memorabilia from the archives of some of our families. Old maps, brochures, notebooks, bills, official records and documents have provided me with additional links to the past. I am indebted to BOB BERGS, GEORGE ERD-MANN, LEONARD GIOVANNOLI, PHIL and CHRIS KELLER, and JUDY KOCH for sharing such items with me.

I am very grateful to those who provided extensive collections of family photographs. Their generosity allowed me to select pictures to illustrate many details of our history. LEONARD GIOVANNOLI, before his death, loaned me two albums and most of the pictures from before 1930 are his. Almost all the pictures of life following that date belong to the collections of six families: DONOVAN, ERDMANN, FRENCH, McDONALD, READ, and WILSON. I have been able to supplement these illustrations with a limited number of additional photographs, thanks to the generosity of almost every one of the authors (or their families) listed above. Photographs that I have chosen for inclusion are identified by number in the text and in the captions. The first digit of each refers to the chapter for which the picture provides an illustration. The remaining numbers identify individual photographs. Reid Wilson, with the assistance of Stuart Kenn of KennKart Digital Mapping, produced the current maps of our region. Their contributions are greatly appreciated.

I thank SHIRLEY McCONNELL and PATRICIA DONOVAN for their help in editing. If any problems remain, I am the one responsible as I am for any errors of fact. All of us owe thanks to those who transformed our contributions into this book, JANE ESCHWEILER and K. P. DONOVAN. I am very grateful to them for helping me endure this difficult process!

Finally, I want to thank PETE McDONALD for his art that enriches us, for his suggestion that initiated the effort to compile this history, and, most of all, for his friendship over some 65 years that has brightened my summers. I am even grateful to him for the gentle prodding over the years to get on with this project—at least I am now that it is finished at last!

Gladys Dickey's map of B918 (see page 84).

1:1. Our NW frontier — "Turning Rock" near Carolyn Island

CHAPTER ONE

Community Defined

The first problem I faced in this study was that of definition. Which families are, or were, part of the community? Do their islands form a coherent geographical unit? This problem is reflected in disagreements over the name or names to be used to designate our region and uncertainties about whether or not any one or another family was closely enough associated with others to justify their inclusion. For example, in his initial response to my inquiries, Leonard Giovannoli noted that his contacts with those whose islands are north and west of French's Bay had not been close. And that same group of islands is sometimes referred to as being on "Mud Channel" and sometimes as being part of "Gronkwa"(spelled "Gronkuwa" on Olver Reid's map of 1915). Without doubt the term "Mud Channel" should refer specifically to the winding shallow channel that separates island 500 A from E 54 (Big Island to all of us, but Shawanaga Island on official maps), a channel extending south of Hole-in-the-Wall to the shallow bay

behind E 3. This channel passes, for much of its extent, through a
muddy marsh and, during years of low lake levels, is virtually
impassable. Gronkwa, on the other hand, seems to have been an
alternate name for Frederic Inlet south of our region. Any confusion
with our islands probably stems from Olver Reid's map on which
the letter "G" of Gronkwa is placed on island B 934, north of
French's Bay, and the term "Gronkuwa Ids" (sic) seems to be applied
to all the islands south of 500 A. Neither name is really appropriate
for our group of islands.

By being forced to confront the problem of geographical limits in order to compile this history, I have realized that indeed there
is a discrete grouping despite the lack of any name for it. There are
limits both to the north and to the south which set our islands apart.
That we are so set apart some of my strongest early memories con-
firm. The repetition of my childhood experience over the years since
reinforces my conviction. Always there is an element of adventure in
reaching our island because one is forced to go "out around
Carolyn" to get there. And to go out around Carolyn Island is to venture into the open waters of Georgian Bay. All other islands between
Carolyn and Pointe au Baril can be reached via deep water channels
protected from the full fury of the waves rolling in from the "open"
as we learned to call the waters to our west. There is no deep water
channel by which our islands can be reached from the north and
west without venturing out from behind sheltering islands. It was
always impressed upon me as a boy that it was this isolation which
set us apart from the "Ojibway folk" and that ours was a special daring which enabled us to settle islands so undesirable to those of a
more timid disposition. In the early days this isolation could be quite
real as well as psychological (See Helen Grove's entry, below). Since
storms could cut us off, we found security in the sight of row upon
row of cans of food upon our shelves, insurance against weather's
worst. Carolyn Island, then, is our NW frontier and the actual border post is that red triangle on "Turning Rock (fig. 1:1)." Once
around that shoal headed home we turned our bows east and the
cresting swells from the west lifted our small craft in an exhilarating
rhythm that brought us back to safety far from the sheets of spray
encountered on the outward journey. This short stretch of water,
dubbed "the bumpy road" by my daughter when, as a little girl, she

first realized its terrors, continues to be a natural barrier in low water. Today, however, in high water small boats can make their way behind Carolyn, thanks to the blasting of the rocks to form "Bedspring Channel" that connects Hemlock Channel to the bay between Windward and Carolyn. Now those who venture into our region need experience only a hint of those earlier terrors and now our isolation is only a memory.

While not as formidable, there is a similar natural barrier south of us. There is a series of sandbars that almost completely closes off Frederic Inlet midway between Shawanaga and the open Georgian Bay. These bars, especially in low water, cut us off from the outside world almost as effectively as did the great waves to the north. This was a route less traveled as the distances between our islands and the sources of supply, the Ojibway and Pointe au Baril, were greater if one had to go south through Frederic Inlet before turning north once again in Shawanaga Bay. Possibly the term, Gronkwa, should properly be applied only to that stretch of the inlet south of these sandbars. At any rate, Leonard Giovannoli speaks of Gronkwa as "the sandy channel." Frederic Inlet is thus divided into two sections by this sand. On one side the islanders have easy access to Shawanaga and, depending on wind direction, a somewhat sheltered run to the mainland. To the north, however, access is more tricky, although now clearly marked channels have reduced the challenges presented by the physical features and the sense of separation. As a child I always felt that we lived between Scylla and Charybdis, between the terrors of open water or those of possible irreparable damage to our propeller, as we tried to thread our way through these little known reefs and bars.

Our group of islands, then, can be defined as those south of Carolyn Island and north of the sandbars in Frederic Inlet. No one name has ever been applied to them, but they are distinctive nonetheless. To the east the unoccupied wilderness of two huge islands, 500 A and E 54, form a barrier as does the open water of Georgian Bay to the west. The sense of being cut off, isolated, created by these natural barriers had much to do with the development of our particular ethos and to our conviction that we inhabited a wilderness area as contrasted with those whose islands were more accessible, surrounded always by other inhabited islands.

Our group of islands is, in turn, subdivided by still another natural feature, French's Bay. This larger body of water was not, and is not, a barrier of the same magnitude as those that form our northern and southern frontiers and is relatively easily crossed in almost any weather by today's motorboats. In the days when almost all short distances were navigated in canoes or rowboats, however, the crossing of French's Bay was not to be undertaken lightly. "Whitecaps on French's Bay" always means a stiff west wind and even a moderate wind can turn the crossing into a stiff 20 minute ordeal in a canoe. I have had to take the motorboat out to rescue my children, Kevin and Maura Grace, trapped in their canoe on the farther shore by wind and wave and before them I remember my sister, Didge, being prevented by the same forces from paddling back across the Bay. This body of water has had the effect of creating two subgroups in our community. There were, and are, some differences between the two as the following accounts will reveal. Some of the islanders south and east of French's Bay look more to the other inhabitants of the islands in Frederic Inlet, while others, particularly those on islands directly adjacent to French's, seem more closely akin to those to the north. There are historical as well as physical reasons for these differences and it is to these I must now turn.

The purchase of islands and the construction of summer cottages in our region is a phenomenon that began in Frederic Inlet and proceeded north. The first such construction began outside our group on the far side of the sandbars and was a summer camp for adults, Reid's Islander Camps, constructed a few years after Beattie's survey of the islands of the entire archipelago in 1911 resulted in the system of island numbering still in use. This survey signals the beginning of the acquisition of island property by private individuals.

The Reid family played an important role in the life of the region around Pointe au Baril. Babs Wilson provides a summary of the family history:

> In the early 1900s Allan Wilson's great uncle, James Reid, and Allan's uncle, Olver Reid, came to Pointe au Baril from Oshawa, Ontario where they had a carriage business. They operated the Pointe au Baril Transfer Business for the Canadian Pacific Railway. In those days there were very few cottages and the three hotels,

Skerryvore, Ojibway and Bellvue, catered to most visitors. J.M. and J.O. Reid looked after two boats—"the Osso" which took passengers for Skerryvore, Ojibway Hotel and intervening cottages, and the large gas boat "Islander" which plied between Pointe au Baril village, MacIntosh Island, Bellevue Hotel, Bowerans, and all cottage calls by the way. Later, when Allan's parents visited, he, then a boy accompanied them. When he was a teenager, Allan came for the summer and worked on the boats for his Uncle Olver, thereby getting to know the whole area.

J.O. (Olver) Reid prepared the chart of the Pointe au Baril group from survey plans of the Georgian Bay Littoral and from personal charting of the area by canoe. This map is the one still used today. We have the original map, now very fragile.

(Eventually, when the highway came in to Pointe au Baril, J.M. and J.O. Reid became Reids' Marine with a taxi boat for passengers and a work boat for hauling cement, lumber, groceries, furniture and anything else people needed for their cottages.)

The earliest inhabitants within our region remained near Olver Reid's establishment; indeed he built for them the earliest cottages, patterned after those of his camp. Those years just before and at the start of World War I, 1913 to 1915, saw the rapid growth of this nucleus. An examination of the gazeteer at the end of this history will reveal the pattern. Individuals, many of whom were introduced to the area as guests at the Islander Camps, either at the end of their first or second summer purchased islands and commissioned Reid to build small cottages on the pattern of the "Klondike" cabins of his camp. Some were school teachers, Miss Fuller from Toronto who purchased B 935 (Nokomis) and Miss Florence Diehl B 945 (Minne-ha-ha, as it is spelled on Reid's map). The Rev. E. Burgess Brown purchased B 944 (Rumwabewin), although he erected no cottage, but presumably camped on his island. Mr. C. G. French from Toronto acquired B 937 (Sagastaweekee). All these islands had been purchased and some had cottages by the summer of 1914. Before that year was out Miss Carrie Zahn from Buffalo had purchased B 919 (Inverurie) and spent her first summer there after marrying Chester Bartow in 1915. In August 1915 still another school teacher, Lucy A. Young from St. Louis purchased B 918.

Since so many families in our little community of islanders were first introduced to this area by two pioneers, Lucy A. Young and Paul Pope, they occupy a special place in this account. Lucy, as members of my family always referred to her, was a very large lady with a great sense of humor. Stories about her and quotations of her funny quips formed a part of my earliest memories of Georgian Bay. Late in her life Gladys Dickey recalled her friend in letters written to me in 1977:

> We all owe a lot to that intrepid old friend of mine, Lucy. A book ought to be written about her. She must have been a thorn in the flesh to her orthodox mother and sister. She left their home fairly early for her own apartment and complete freedom. Her second trip to Europe was leading a group of tourists...and I'll bet those who went under her leadership never forgot her. She always taught beginning second grade—and was a wizard with children. She made 2 + 2 hilarious and a primer a delight. Eccentric, independent, and delightful right to the end.

> I often relive some evenings in a boat on placid water as the sun was about to disappear out in the west—or early mornings on my back porch when the birds began to voice their morning greetings—and I think how fortunate I was to know someone like Lucy with whom I spent part of two summers in her cottage. I wonder if Charles Anderson still occupies his cottage across her bay? Lucy was someone you would never dream would like such a place; I remember painting in the name of her island on a bare spot as I left for St. Louis. She never roughed it—no camping out for her—after her first summer there in Reid's Camp she lost no time picking out her island and arranging for its building. Her cottage was as comfortable and well-equipped as her St. Louis apartment. Her faithful maid, Anna, came with her.

> The last time she came on a brief visit (probably 1947, the year the island changed owners, ed.) wasn't sad. She stayed with me and every day we went to her cottage to pack up her personal belongings before she turned it over to the new owners. It never was sad with Lucy for we spent time giggling over the funny times there. In Toronto once she had just purchased a pair of shoes. On going out she discovered it was raining. She had discarded her old shoes so she tucked the new ones under her arm and proceeded to her Toronto hotel in stocking feet.

Our "foundation myth" is the story of how, in 1915, Lucy went to the ticket counter at the Union Station in St. Louis and asked the clerk for a railroad ticket to "someplace far, far away." He sold her a ticket to Pointe au Baril where she was a guest at Reid's Islander Camps. Afterwards she told of a fellow teacher and friend who accompanied her on that trip. This woman had very long hair which she used to comb out and arrange over the covers when she went to bed. To her great consternation, one night a deer mouse, exploring the cabin, became entangled in her hair. This was the first mouse story in our community but certainly not the last. Every family has its tale of these attractive, but pesky, creatures! By August of that year, before she left, Lucy had purchased her island.

The following year, 1916, Lucy invited two other teachers from her school in St. Louis to visit her in her new cottage. One was my aunt, Gladys Dickey. On another visit Gladys and another teacher, Helen Whitelaw, discovered the island E 5. Gladys recalled that discovery in a letter much later.

> Lucy it was who told Helen and me that someone had told her E 5 was a nice island. So one morning Helen and I paddled up, turned into Pope's narrow channel and made our first entrance into our little bay. We found E 5 after a little difficulty for it looked like a part of its neighboring big island. And we liked it. And bought it.

The date of that first visit to E 5 was probably 1922, for it was in that year that the two women actually purchased the island. The cottage was constructed in 1924 and they spent their first summer in it in 1926. Through Gladys Dickey the Donovan and Erdmann clans were introduced to the islands in 1930 and 1931; they now own E 3, E 27, and B 980. Through Helen Whitelaw another teacher at her school, Roosevelt High School in St. Louis, Walter E. Riley, decided to purchase B 995 (Belle Chasse) in 1928. We were always told the romantic tale that Mr. Riley was enamored of Helen, but that she did not return his love, so he bought this island from which he could gaze at the object of his affections from afar. This island is currently owned by Mr. Riley's stepson, Bob Bergs. Still other friends of Helen Whitelaw, Reuben and Eleanor Read, purchased E 27 in 1933 (now owned by Maura Donovan and David Whitman). The Reads were associated with Principia College in Elsah, Illinois, near St. Louis. All these families, thus, reached our region through the spark ignited by Lucy Young and all originally had ties to St. Louis, 1000 miles away. This Missouri invasion began from island B 918 in the southern part of our domain.

Others came from the north, from the Ojibway area, thanks to Paul R. Pope and his wife Elfrieda. Paul Pope was professor of German at Cornell University in Ithaca, New York. Elfrieda's parents had emigrated from Germany and settled in Chicago. She retained a love of Germany all her life which made the period of both World Wars difficult for her and her husband. He was as eccentric in his way as Lucy Young. I worked for him each summer when I was in my teens doing odd jobs and helping him open and close his cottage. He saved everything. On his back porch, carefully arranged on hooks, were bits of string, wire, and other miscellany. For an ice box the Popes used an old trunk stuffed with straw for insulation in an effort to slow the melting of the small piece of ice. Mice loved that straw and it was always an adventure to open the trunk! He threatened to discourage unwelcome boaters near his island by flitting from tree to tree dressed only in his long underwear—a threat which I am sure would discourage no one today! He was a popular raconteur at picnics. We children encouraged him to retell his many, lengthy anecdotes. And he was a musician. I can never paddle near his island without hearing in my mind's ear the sound of his violin coming across the water at sunset from the porch of Fayola.

The Popes had been guests at the Ojibway Hotel and, before the end of summer, 1919, had purchased two islands, Minnisabik near the Ojibway on Ugo Igo Channel and, in the remote area south of Carolyn, B 987 (Fayola) now owned by the Kochs. Through the Popes all the New York, New Jersey, and Ohio members of our community were introduced to these islands. In 1929 Dr. Pope invited a fellow language teacher, Ethel Williams, professor of Spanish at Western Reserve University in Cleveland and daughter of one of his colleagues on the faculty of Cornell, to vacation on Minnisabik. She in turn purchased E 18 (Chinook) now owned by the Franklins. Ethel brought up first as guests and then fellow islanders, Helen Lewandowski and Clinton Grove who were married on the island they purchased, B 985. From the Groves and their guests, the Foutz family, the present clans of Groves, Kochs, Malones, Franklins, and Hofmanns derive today owning islands E 5, E 18, B 985, and B 987. The Hofmanns, in turn, introduced a faculty colleague, Dudley Curry and his wife Fran, to our area. They purchased island B 921 and now own the Bartow island, B 919, as well. Ethel also brought up members of her own family, her nephews and niece, Dix, Pete, and Mary Ellen McDonald. The latter, together with her husband, Elbert Baker, now owns B 1000 and part of B 937, while Pete and Linda McDonald own the other half of that island.

There are currently 17 islands in our area on which cottages have been built. Of this number six were at one time, or still are, occupied by those connected directly or indirectly with Lucy Young. Paul Pope and those introduced to the area by him purchased another four. Nine of the ten islands whose owners can be traced to Young and Pope lie north of French's Bay. To the north the ownership of B 979 provides the only exception having been purchased by a family from Ottawa. The seven islands with cottages of our group south of French's Bay present a different picture. Those individuals whose initial visit was to Reid's Camps or the Ojibway Hotel were often the first to buy and build in this part of our area and they came either from Missouri (Young), New York (Bartow and Diehl), or directly from Toronto (French and Fuller). Now, however, three of the seven are occupied by those indirectly connected to Young or Pope.

There are chronological differences in the development of ownership and cottage-building as well as those that stem from location or from the way in which individuals first came to the area. An historian can define several distinct periods. First is the period from just prior to World War I until approximately 1920, marked by the occupation of the islands in the southern group and a flurry of cottage building there. The islands with cottages built in this first period are B 918 (Young), B 919 (Bartow), B 935 (Fuller), B 937 (French), and B 945 (Diehl).

There were other islands purchased and built upon in this southern region during the first period which do not figure in this history as they lie very close to, or just beyond, our band of sandbars and their occupants for whatever reason had less contact with those whose stories are included here. These islands are B 856 (recently owned by Graham and Maja Willoughby who first came to the area as guests of George and Sue Erdmann on E 3), B 857, B 858 & 859 (now owned by Beverly & Sally Spaethe) and B 867 (Phyllis Spaethe). During this period Charles H. Anderson acquired B 857 and built a cottage, boat house, and ice house. He was an important figure during the first and second periods as he had a motorboat and provided water taxi services to the other islanders for many years. At one end of this island two brothers, Mose and Felix Laramie, from Penetanguishene finally built a small log cabin which is still standing. They had originally lived each summer on the boat they motored up in. For many years, extending into he next period, they were the carpenters, masons, and dock builders in the southern region .

During this first period, too, there seems to have been some purchase of islands for speculative or investment purposes. Anderson himself purchased, or bought options, on several (e.g. B 924) as did Olver Reid. The latter purchased B 921 in 1928 (listed in his father's name) and built a cottage which seems never to have been used. In 1919, on the SW side of French's Bay B 962 was purchased by the Ives family of New York (now in California). They had a cement floor and a handsome stone fireplace built which has given the island its popular name, "Fireplace," to us, although it is called Divided Island on the official maps. No cottage was ever completed, nor has the island ever been occupied, although the owners have camped there on occasion; they continue to hold it as an investment. Still farther north, as early as 1913 F. C. Carter purchased B 995, but nothing was built on the island until Riley bought it in 1928. In 1919 Pope bought B 987, but did not build on it during this period. During this first period there were no cottages at all in the northern half of our area.

At this time there was a law requiring that, in order to hold an island, an improvement worth at least $500 had to be made. Hence the mysterious cottage on B 921 and the stonework on B 962. However, some islands were held for years without any such improvement, so the law was not uniformly enforced.

Even during this first period changes began to take place. Reid's Camps closed and property in the southern group began to change hands. For example, Harry Giovannoli, a newspaper man from Kentucky with a passion for fishing purchased Florence Diehl's

"Minnie-ha-ha" (B 945). He had been a guest at the Ojibway Hotel in 1908 and brought his family, after the death of his first wife, to Reid's Camps in 1915. After buying B 945 in 1920 Giovannoli renamed the island "Kenusa" which is explained in Leonard's account below.

My second period extends from 1920 to the end of the decade, to the crash of the U.S. stock market in 1929. This decade was the golden age, in many ways, for the original settlers in the southern region: many cottages were enlarged or improved and some new ones built. The photographs reveal communal picnics, swimming, and even religious services held out of doors on one of the islands. During this period the first cottages were constructed in the northern section. The pride of place for the first cottage there goes to the Popes who returned from a trip to Germany in the summer of 1923 in time to pay a visit to their newly constructed abode on Fayola. They had purchased the island in 1919, but did not build until 1923. Already, in the preceding summer, Helen Whitelaw and Gladys Dickey had purchased E 5 but, being impecunious teachers, could not afford to build on the island until 1924. In fact during this decade Gladys augmented her income by working most summers at a teahouse in Door County, Wisconsin. It was not until 1926 that Helen and Gladys visited their new cottage for the first time. The two cottages on that little bay were joined by a third in 1928 when Mr. Riley acquired Carter's Belle Chasse. Throughout this period there were not enough islanders in this northern section to form any sort of a community. It is clear from Leonard's photographs that the ladies continued to associate closely with the cottagers to the south and, presumably, the Popes continued their association with their neighbors near Minnisabik and the Ojibway.

During the third period, after the stock market crash to the end of World War II, the situation changed dramatically. In terms of new cottage construction this third period was to the northern section what the first period had been to the southern. In 1930 Ethel Williams built on Chinook (E 18) directly across the bay from the Pope's cottage on Fayola. The following year Helen and Clint Grove's cottage was in place on B 985 and they were married there the end of the summer, 1931, an event which was to be a high point in our island lore. It was the first wedding ever celebrated here in our islands and only a few have followed their example in the many years since then. In 1933 (the purchase registered in December, 1932) Reuben and Eleanor Read built on E 27, an island they named "Peace." That same year the Donovans had B 980 surveyed, but did not actually have a cottage ready for occupancy until the summer of 1934. One wonders if the delay might have been caused by the arrival of a new member of the family, Didge, in 1933? Gladys Dickey contributed to her sister and brother-in-law's domain by having a small bunk house built on the same island.

The construction of this bunk house on the Donovan property suggests that there were pressures for space on E 5 and that Gladys needed to find a new summer location. Helen's redoubtable mother, Kate, was apparently bothered by visitors. She was already very elderly having been a little girl in Minnesota during the Sioux uprising of 1862. I was much impressed as a little boy when she demonstrated the dances of the Sioux at a picnic! Gladys, on the other hand, lived for visitors and both the Erdmanns in 1930 and the Donovans in 1931 had visited her on E 5. The solution was for Helen and Gladys to give up joint ownership. Late in 1936 a parcel at the front of E 3 was purchased by the two women, although it was listed in Kate's name. There in 1937 Gladys erected a simple cottage, one room with two small sleeping porches. Helen would retain E 5 and Gladys accepted E 3 in return for her interest in the other. That same year Ethel Williams purchased B 1000 and put up a guest cottage there. After 1937 no new cottages were built in our area until after World War II.

Not only was the third period a time of island purchases and cottage building, it was also a time for the second generation to spend their childhood summers here. The earlier settlers had been adults, to be sure sometimes young adults, when their summers as cottagers in Georgian Bay began, but in the 1930s youngsters, too, joined the population. The Giovannoli boys, Leonard and Robert, although their first visits had been as teenagers, were of college age before they were regular summer occupants. The Bartow's son Chet, born in 1918, grew up spending many summers here.

Most of this younger generation lived north of French's Bay during the 1930s. Since many of these youngsters are now the adult owners of these same islands, a brief summary is in order. The three McDonalds of Shaker Heights, Ohio, were regular summer guests on the island of their aunt, Ethel Williams. In 1929 Dix, the eldest, spent several weeks with Ethel on Minnisabik which the Popes had invited her to use. Ethel invited Dix's younger sister, Brownie, to join them after the cottage was built on Chinook in 1930. Finally the third sibling, Pete, made his first visit in 1935. The Erdmann boys, Jim and George, came first with their father and their mother, who was a sister of Gladys Dickey, as guests on E 5 during the summer of 1930 and in the following summer Gladys's other sister, Dorothy, came with her husband and three sons, Dick, Bob, and me. I was eighteen months old. While clearly the Donovan family had a wonderful time that summer, my father did not rush to buy an island. The following year we tried a cottage on Michigan's Drummond Island in the North Channel, but the water, I was told, was too cold for my father to swim in with comfort, so that fall he had Island B 980 surveyed. In 1934 all the Donovans, Erdmanns, and Gladys Dickey summered on the newly acquired island, the fathers, Elmer Donovan and Morris Erdmann with the four older boys in the main cottage, the three sisters, Gladys, Gwen, and Dorothy together with me and my new sister, Didge (known during that first year of her life simply as "Baby Sister") in the Bunk House.

In this second generation, the oldest were three boys, Dix McDonald, Dick Donovan, and Jim Erdmann, and one girl, Betsy Read, the only child of Reuben and Eleanor Read on E 27. A few years younger were George Erdmann, Bob Donovan, and Brownie McDonald (now Baker). Pete and I were too young to run with these lively teens and yet old enough to feel superior to the girls who, born after 1930, joined the community as infants, Didge and Betsy Donovan (who was just 3 months old when she arrived for her first summer) and Nancy and Judy Grove (now Malone and Koch respectively). The youngest member of this second generation, Clint Grove, Jr., arrived after the war.

Most of the younger members of this generation reached their teens following World War II. During the war itself few of us were able to reach the islands for any summer vacation. 1941 was our last summer before the United States entered the war. Despite gasoline rationing, my family managed a few weeks in 1944. Carrie Bartow records in her diary of 1943 that the Bartows were the only inhabitants in Frederic Inlet that summer. By 1946, however, things began to return to normal.

The following period, the fourth in our story, from 1946 to 1962, was a time of transitions. There was a change in our whole way of life caused by the rapid increase in prosperity in the post war years. There were improvements in the roads leading northward to Pointe au Baril. Automobiles became more comfortable and capable of ever higher speeds and of pulling boats on trailers. Almost everyone, it seemed, now owned an outboard motor. No longer did what we had always thought of as wilderness seem so far removed from the growing metropolis, Toronto. No longer were our islands of Georgian Bay to be the sole preserve of cottagers, for now all were within reach of the outboard motorboats which brought eager fishermen even out around Carolyn to our bays and channels. The almost awesome silence, formerly broken only by wind, wave, and birds, was replaced by the racket of motors, a sound which soon became as omnipresent as the summer sound of the gasoline-powered lawn mowers in the cities and suburbs from which we liked to think we could escape. To this motorized cacophony was added the roar of airplanes. In 1949 my father and his friend, Dr. Ted Jean, chartered an amphibious plane in Gravenhurst which brought them to a safe landing in French's Bay. This was an exciting first and was duly noted as such in Carrie's diary. It was a harbinger of the airplanes no longer chartered but based at the islands of Baker and Wilson.

If what had before seemed remote and wild became accessible to more and more people thanks to these developments, our daily lives were being transformed by others. Septic tanks, at least for a time, promised to end one perennial problem for those who dwell on rocky islands! Propane made possible more reliable stoves and ovens, but the greatest wonder of all was refrigeration powered either by propane or kerosene. At last our diet no longer depended so heavily on cans. Cold drinks could refresh whenever the weather became hot instead of only on the day ice was brought back from the Ojibway!

While these transitions in patterns of cottage life were significant, in some ways our memories recall the transitions involving persons with greater vividness. During these two decades old friends gradually stopped coming and sold or passed on their islands to younger people. It was a time when the second generation grew up and produced a third generation of children to enjoy Georgian Bay summers. And it was a time when newcomers were introduced to our community. A major loss at the very beginning of the period was that of Dix McDonald killed in an accident in Colorado. We lost one whose interest in the flora of our region, in his case scientific, characterizes so many in our community. It is no accident that his younger brother, Pete, edits the "Ojibway Naturalist." Like so many of our number Dix loved the observation and recording of nature, not the trophies of rod, reel, and gun. Also early in this period the Reads, one of the original families, ended their tenure on E 27 after Reuben's death. Their simple cabin soon became derelict until George and Sue Erdmann, after purchasing the island in 1957, removed its remains (where the Bunk House now stands) and built a new cottage on a different site. Lucy Young, too elderly in 1947 for the rigors of cottage life, sold her island. Paul Pope died in 1950 after a long and distinguished academic career. With his death we lost a vast treasure of island lore. An increase in the number of motorboats caused Ethel Williams, now married to Sam Plimpton, to sell her island in 1947. She could no longer tolerate the changes these post war years had brought to the formerly quiet waters. She sold to the Foutz family, friends of Helen Grove, from Tiffin, Ohio. With Ethel's departure the whistle that summoned her island's guests to a morning dip was silenced and no longer were we to see her familiar Peterborough "Kawartha" set out from the back of Chinook on its run to the Ojibway. In 1946 Mr Riley's wife drowned off the front of his island and, grief-stricken, he transferred the ownership to his stepson, Bob Bergs, in 1947. Another familiar sight of our childhood would now be seen only in memory—the old rowboat being propelled by Mr Riley facing the stern and pushing, rather than pulling, the oars so that he could see where he was going. Other departures during the 1950s included Helen Whitelaw whose periods of acute depression forced an end in 1953 to a long number of active summers. Any witnesses will never forget her truly awesome dives, belly flops, which never failed to produce giggles from irreverent children. And all children here were the poorer when Gladys Dickey decided that, when all she was physically capable of was chores, it was time to bring an end to her island ownership and give E 3 to her sister, Gwen Erdmann. Fortunately she continued to come as a guest for many visits so that still another generation knew "Aunt Gladys" at the island and learned the wonders of nature through her love and enthusiasm. The 1960s brought other losses. Clint Grove died leaving forever unfinished his dream, the stone cottage he had begun on the front of their island. My father made his last visit during the cold, wet summer, 1964; he died the following spring. 1964 marked the last year of island ownership by Leonard Giovannoli. Over his many summers here he had become almost a legendary figure to us, the source of so much information about the natural world. No longer would he guide us to beaver lodges, rarely to be seen in those years as a result of over-trapping. No longer would he be available to identify the species of animal we had found, nor answer our questions about rigging a canoe for sailing. Through his quiet ways and gentle humor he appears to us today to represent a model for one in harmony with the world of summer in Georgian Bay. Fortunately he, too, made several later visits before his death in 1994.

This time of transition also witnessed the childhood of the third generation. All the second generation from before the war were married by this time and had families of their own. Both spouses and a new generation of children were now introduced to the island. George and Sue Erdmann brought their three, Molly, Gwen, and David, to enjoy the newly built cottage on E 27. Dick and Mildred Donovan with their three, Mike, Steve, and Susan, together with Bob and Hope Donovan and their three, Faith, Peter, and Brian, stretched the capacity of Eagle Island as it is still being stretched to this day! The Bakers began to raise their five, Buff, Wendy, Nancy, Martha, and Tim, in the ever expanding cottage on B 1000, formerly known as Battleship. The Frenches made radical changes at Sagastaweekee enjoyed by the three children, John, Sandra, and Gary. For us, the younger members of that older generation, this time of transition offered few opportunities for island summers. We were off finishing college, serving in the armed forces, going abroad, getting started on careers. It would not be until the late 1960s or early 1970s that we would become again regulars with our own children to add to the summer population.

Finally, this time of transition brought new families into our community. Helen Grove invited as a guest Gertrude (Dickie) Foutz who, in turn, introduced her brother Ralph and his wife Dorothy.

They purchased Chinook in 1947 sight unseen from Ethel Williams Plimpton and came with their daughters Molly and Jean who joined with the Donovan and Grove girls to form the teenage set in the early 1950s. The Foutz family, a few years later, in 1953, also purchased E 5 from Helen Whitelaw when, so the story has it, she threw boiling water on some creature in her garbage pail only to discover that it was a skunk! The next day she posted a notice at the Ojibway that the island was for sale. Thus the Foutz family came to own two islands. Other additions to our community were Allan Wilson, his wife Babs, sons Peter and Reid, who purchased B 952, crown land in French's Bay, late in 1959. Here, in a sense, our story comes full circle because Allan was a nephew of Olver Reid whose island camp more than 40 years earlier had served to introduce so many to our region. The expansion of our community through the purchase of unoccupied islands came to an end when the sale of crown land ceased. The last one to be acquired was B 979 SW of Eagle Island. Here W. A. Tiffin, whose daughter married into the family of Pointe au Baril contractor John Hodgson, erected a small cottage in 1963 to be used for hunting and fishing. It was unlike others, both because it was seldom occupied during the summer months, and because of its unusual blue flat roof which gave rise to such appellations as "Dairy Queen" or "Hot Dog Stand"!

After 1963 new families joined our community only when islands already owned were put up for sale. In this way Fran and Dudley Curry and their son Eric acquired B 921 in 1969. This small island had first been registered as owned by James McBain Reid, Olver's father, and a cottage, never occupied, had been erected in 1925 to hold it. The ruins of this cottage precariously perched on a lofty rock, a landmark during my childhood, were then torn down and replaced with a new cottage more securely sited farther back from the water. Another new family, Tom and Shirley McConnell with daughters Lisa and Nancy, acquired B 979 in 1990, removed the "Hot Dog Stand" (except for its outhouse) and transformed the appearance of that island.

All the other changes in ownership during this present period after 1963 have been simply the transfer from one member of our community to another. Judy Grove and her husband Heintz Koch purchased Fayola from Elfrieda Pope Bestelmeyer in 1974; the Foutz family in 1965 transferred ownership of their two islands to their daughters, E 18 to Molly and her husband Jim Franklin and E 5 to Jean and her husband David Hofmann. In 1975 John H. Watson inherited B 935 upon the death of his aunt, Peggy Hamilton. E 3 passed from the Erdmann family to Steve Donovan, Dick's son, and his wife Sarah in 1986. Still earlier, in 1982, B 937, the original French island, was acquired by Pete and Linda McDonald together with his sister and brother-in-law, Brownie and Bake Baker. In 1986 the widow of Chet Bartow, Jr., Carrie's son, passed ownership of B 919 to the Curry family. The last transfer, up to this date, was in 1997 when George and Sue Erdmann sold E 27 to David Whitman and Maura Donovan.

By the mid 1960s those of us younger members of the second generation, now grown up and settled, began to introduce our spouses and children of the third generation to cottage life. During the late 1960s and 1970s the younger members of the third generation included Kevin and Maura Donovan, Marcie and Andy McDonald (much later to be joined by step brothers, Todd and Brad Sanders), Wendy, Steve, Jill, Margo, Kevin, and Chris Malone, and Nanci (Pooh) and Andrew Koch. Later still, but for a short time only, Clint Grove, Jr.'s daughter Heather was included in this number.

Newcomers during the 1950s and 1960s also added to the number of children and teenagers growing up during this present period. There were Reid Wilson on B 952 and Eric Curry on B 921 and later B 919. In the northern group of islands there were four young Franklins, Bill, Mike, Linda, and Eva and five Hofmann children, Steve, Lisa, Laura, Kurt, and Karla.

Not surprisingly, given the growing numbers in our families in this present period, there has been much remodeling of existing cottages, the addition of many new bunk houses, and even the subdivision of some properties permitting additional cottages to be built. There are very few islands, indeed, where such construction has not taken place over the past 20 years, the details of which may be found later in the gazeteer concluding this work.

Now as a new century begins one may note the portents of changes coming. Already the first children of still another generation have made their appearance and it is for them that this history is being written. Increasing numbers will continue to add to the pressure on our cottages for space and for time in the years ahead. The coming years will also be another time of transition. Those of the second generation, some of whom already are no longer to be found of a summer in familiar places, will soon be passing their cottages on to their heirs. Some islands will be sold and newcomers added. Other changes are difficult to predict. One thing will remain the same, however. There will continue to be those who love this region, who will inherit our traditions here recorded, and strive to pass them on, and who will one day add their own chapters to this account.

2:2. Start of the long drive to Pointe au Baril.
Leonard Giovannoli ready to leave Kentucky in the 1920s

CHAPTER TWO

Challenges and Pleasures of Island Life

Any summary of our community and summers on our islands requires some discussion of the mechanics of living. To some extent all aspects of our life were, and continue to be, affected by such details and some of the changes mentioned in the previous chapter were influenced by the changes outlined below. The basic problems that our cottagers confront remain constant; only the attempted solutions vary and, it seems to me now, that each new solution, while it may resolve an old problem, introduces new complications. In many ways our life is no easier today than it was earlier, but it is different. Our problems arise from the fact that these islands are remote, are inhospitable to human life, and their fragile environment is threatened by human occupation, especially by the end products, both organic and inorganic, of that occupation.

The remoteness of our location causes problems for travel and for communication. How does one get to the island? Once there, how does one communicate with the outside world? How does one get necessary supplies of food and fuel? Finally, how does one dispose of waste on rocky islands with no possibility of digging pits for its burial? The answers to these questions change over the years, but the questions remain the same.

The first cottagers in our area arrived each summer by train from Toronto either to Parry Sound or to Pointe au Baril. At that time it was called "the Station" to distinguish it from "the Village," the small community at the lighthouse. The station proper was up on the hill just south of the trestle. Many a story is told of the struggle to hike up that steep roadway from the government wharf below lugging suitcases growing heavier with each step! The railroad was the Canadian Pacific; it advertised vacations at Pointe au Baril during the 1920s. Many of us still treasure the brochures. There were two trains each way daily, one during daylight hours and one at night. For me the smell of the preservative once used on railway ties immediately evokes my earliest memories of the station. When I was very small I rarely made the trip by train; it was too expensive for a large family. My mother and younger sisters and sometimes my father traveled that way. In 1946, however, I came up by the day train and, in order to reach the dining car, I had to pass through the parlor car with its individual, swivel armchairs. Then I had to stand in line for what seemed like hours before finally being seated for a feast of lamb chops.

A few years later I enjoyed the luxury of a berth in the sleeping car dedicated to this station each weekend. These cars were the old fashioned Pullmans with 12 sections (an upper and a lower berth each) plus a "drawing room" with two beds and an upper berth. Twenty-seven passengers could be accommodated. Every Friday night during the summer a sleeper was brought up and left on a siding so that the weekenders from Toronto could sleep to a civilized hour before getting off while the train which brought them hurtled on through the night towards Sudbury to the north. This same car was then available for boarding early on Sunday evening ready to be picked up once again in the middle of the night by the train to Toronto. I discovered on that trip that many of the regulars left their bottles in the care of the porter so that they might enjoy a libation before retiring for the night! In the morning the many gleaming sinks in the commodious men's lavatory were all in use as the travelers prepared to head directly for their offices for a full day's work the moment the train arrived in Toronto. In railroad literature the description of this "Men's Dressing Room" mentions that it is a "masculine" room whose gender seems to be tied to the fact that it had "big wash basins...dental basin...electric razor outlets," etc. "It is also an ideal room for lounging and smoking." I can not remember whether this particular example still retained the brass spittoons which added to this masculine flavor. The Women's Dressing Room, on the other hand, was characterized in the published descriptions by the fact that it was "sparkling clean at all times...furnished with dressing table, chairs...plenty of soap and hot water, an ample supply of fresh towels and a wealth of well-diffused light."

Still later I made the journey from the north, leaving Sault Ste. Marie on a train to Sudbury late in the afternoon and changing in that city to the southbound train. Unfortunately this train arrived in Pointe au Baril in the middle of the night forcing me to await the dawn in the station waiting room. Those of us returning to St. Louis had a long wait in Toronto between the afternoon arrival from the Pointe and the late night departure of the train to Chicago. We usually spent these hours in the spacious lounges of the Royal York Hotel. In those early years the trains were pulled by steam locomotives. The cars were not air-conditioned. Smoke and soot blew through the open windows. Especially during the war, one could not count on having a dining car on the train. I remember Gladys Dickey telling me of one such trip when the train paused at McTier, south of Pointe au Baril, to allow the passengers to get off for a quick bite at the station buffet. Alas, all she was able to purchase was a piece of raisin pie and she hated raisins! One memory that remains vivid to this day of those trips is of the brilliantly colored flowers so profusely planted around every station on the line. By the early 1960s the stop at Pointe au Baril was dropped and, by a curious reversal, one had to get to Parry Sound by bus or car in order to catch the train there. Travel by train to and from Pointe au Baril is now but a memory.

Since there was no highway to Pointe au Baril until the mid 1930s travelers by car before that time either had to leave their automobiles in Sudbury or Parry Sound and complete the journey by rail, or by boat from Parry Sound. Once the highway was complete, however, the automobile became the usual mode of conveyance (fig. 2:2). The trip was usually long, slow, and hot. Automobiles were primitive by today's standards. I can remember when 50 miles per hour was considered breathtaking speed, 40 or 45 was more usual. Indeed the rural speed limit was officially 35 in 1930-1931! Trucks went even slower and the narrow, two lane highways made passing difficult. It was not unusual to find great lines of cars and trucks one after another slowly moving north on Highway 11. This was the route north which we picked up at Thornhill having crossed by ferry from Port Huron to Sarnia. What a great moment it was to turn north and feel that our island was at last near at hand! Highway 11 was paved, but north of Barrie, whether we came via Gravenhurst or Bracebridge, the roads were gravel. Once on the gravel one had the feeling that civilization had been left behind, the wilderness entered. The thrill of those final miles compensated for the "washboard" effect of that rough surface and the still slower speeds required. In those days a good day's drive was 300 or at most 350 miles. My family usually spent three nights out on the 1000 mile trip from St. Louis to Pointe au Baril.

Before the war motels were very rare indeed. One had the choice of a hotel in the center of towns or cities, usually more expensive, or a tourist home, a forerunner of the present B and B, on a more primitive level. Private baths were unheard of, breakfast rarely provided, although my father always tried to find ones that did—he hated to start driving on an empty stomach! The beds, too, could provide an adventure. I remember at least one where the mattresses were stuffed with corn stalks. On the outskirts of towns one might find tourist cabins, the forerunner of the motel. Even locating accommodation for the night was an adventure. There were no directories of tourist homes, no national number to call to make reservations, almost no advertising along the highways leading into town. We simply drove in and looked for the word, "Tourists," on a sign in front of houses which took in travelers. Needless to say, one encountered many surprises along the way! The second night out we stopped at a tourist home in Stratford, Kitchener, or Guelph and, after the war, following a different route, in Goderich or Kincardine. On the third day we drove to Parry Sound where my family took over much of the top floor at Miss Spence's, an establishment, although much changed, still to be found under the railroad trestle across from the hospital. As a teenager I particularly appreciated the bathtub whose extraordinary length allowed me to luxuriate in the last hot bath before summer's end. We made this stop, so close to our final destination, to avoid arriving at the island late in the day. Opening a cottage always seemed easier in the morning.

The difficulties created by primitive automobiles and rough roads have, since the war, been replaced by the difficulties of more dangerous speeds of the automobiles and the ever increasing congestion, particularly on weekends and holidays. No longer do these roads pass through the center of towns and old number 11 is no longer two lane, nor is it any longer the only route since north of Barrie one can follow the newer multi-laned 400. What has been gained is much easier and more rapid transportation of both people and goods from Toronto and points beyond to our gateway Pointe au Baril. The distance which used to require a day's journey now takes little over three hours. Primitive accommodations have been replaced by far more comfortable ones. What has been lost in the anonymity of the modern motel and franchise restaurant is the contact with the families who owned and operated the earlier establishments. Lost is the adventurous feel to the trip itself which seems now more of a commute. Lost, too, is the remoteness, the sense of wilderness, which so attracted people here in the beginning. It takes effort and planning now to transform the journey to the island from just miles to an adventurous part of the summer's experience it once was.

Our transportation problems were only partially behind us by the time we reached Parry Sound or Pointe au Baril, however. There was, and still is, the boat ride from the mainland to the island. The more remote the island the greater the problem. In the earliest days almost no one had a personal motor-powered boat. To my knowledge, for example, Lucy Young, Helen Whitelaw, Gladys Dickey, Reuben and Eleanor Read, and, at least initially, Clint and Helen Grove neither owned such a boat, nor knew how to operate one. Ernie Pope explains below why his family remained on Minnisabik until the 1920s by the fact that they wanted to be within rowing distance of the nearest source of supply, the Ojibway Hotel. In our first period, then, the pioneers used the commercial steamboat service from Pointe au Baril out to the Ojibway or to one of the other hotels or camps and then hired a smaller gasoline powered

2:3. By water taxi to the island. Parry Sound, 1934. (l. to r.), George Erdmann, Gladys Dickey, Bob Donovan, Jonas, Dick Donovan, Jim Erdmann

boat to transport them the rest of the way. No steamboat, however, could ever come near the remote location of our islands.

The motorboats for hire at the beginning and end of our stay were the only inboards most of us were to ride in during the summer (fig. 2:3). The rarity of return visits to the mainland after we once reached our destination again contributed to the feeling that our islands were isolated. During the 1920s Charles Anderson of Toronto provided this boat livery service to those living in the southern group of islands and his base was very close by on B 857. By the 1930s, however, the closest boats for hire were either at the Station or at the Village. My first memory of the trip out was in the workboat of the local contractor, Thorkildsen. His grey inboard had the usual displacement hull of the powerboats of the period and was, therefore, slower, but provided a more comfortable ride, than modern planing hulls. For a child this ride was one of summer's thrills. Indeed, the ride back to Pointe au Baril in an actual motorboat was the only thing which reconciled me to the thought of leaving the island at summer's end to return to school. At least there was the ride into the Station!

It was not long before some operators specialized in this service of transporting cottagers. In the 1930s some of our islanders patronized Mr. Richardson of the Village whose gleaming white launch had wicker chairs while others preferred Mr. Percy Woodward of the Station who used a mahogany launch with upholstered seats. After the war there were Archie and Edna Taylor who provided this service for most of us. Finally Jerry Evoy, and now his son Shane, at the Station became the one who regularly ferried us to our islands. Many are still dependent upon Evoy to bring them out and to start them later on their homeward way.

Most memories of these trips are of uneventful passages, joyous at the start of the season, sad at the end. Sometimes, however, there are stories of the violent winds and waves encountered on a stormy trip out around Carolyn, or of the hazards of low water navigation and the occasional shoal hit. There have been times when the operators of the service forgot the day or the hour of departure, leaving frustrated passengers sitting beside their luggage on the rock in front of their cottage. Sometimes fog has prevented the expected boat from arriving on schedule. On one memorable occasion one of the, by then, venerable boats of the Ryder brothers (who had taken over from Woodward) began to leak on the run into the Station and passengers and luggage finally arrived quite damp after a hasty transfer into a small boat. Unabashed, the Ryders submitted a bill for this trip only to be sent, in reply, a bill for dry cleaning!

What has been changing over the past few decades is that ever more cottagers are using their own boats for this final leg of the journey. The advantages include a greater freedom to come and go, especially important for those making frequent visits over the summer. With one's own boat, one does not have to wait for a water taxi to become available and can select any suitable hour for the trip to the Station. There are, of course, disadvantages in this shift: the much greater expense involved in acquiring, maintaining, and especially in storing a large and powerful boat and the additional noise and fuel consumption from more boats used more frequently. As we use our boats in the same way we use our automobiles we become commuters in the summer at the island as we are in the cities during the winter.

While the shift to privately owned boats of sufficient size and power to transport a number of people and their luggage at high speed is a recent phenomenon in our group of islands, there were, to be sure, some cottagers who, early on, acquired more modest power-boats. With these boats their owners addressed our second great problem: when people reached the island, how were they to get food and fuel? At first the supplies and the people arrived together and when the former was exhausted, the latter departed. I grew up hearing of orders sent to Michie's, Simpson's, or Eaton's in Toronto, of hampers of food being brought by porters onto the train to accompany their owners north. Gladys Dickey spoke of butter in tubs and bacon packed in salt as a preservative, the supply of both being expected to last for the duration of her stay. When cottagers began travelling by car they sent a large initial order for groceries to C.C. Kennedy's store at the Station to be ready to bring out when they arrived. It was C.C. Kennedy, too, who began to provide a weekly supply boat so that one could count on groceries brought right to one's island. The sight of that large inboard motorboat emerging into French's Bay from between Nokomis (B 935) and Sagastaweekee (B 937) was an exciting moment for me as a little boy (fig. 2:4). An order for the following week was sent in each time the boat stopped. In addition to bringing a prepared order to each cottage Mr. Kennedy carried some fresh produce and a scale so purchases could be made on the spot. Sometimes there were critical comments about quality, but only the disappearance of this service made us all aware of its great convenience. After the war the Ojibway attempted a similar service for a year or two and Archie Taylor kept the tradition of delivery alive through 1952. Thanks to those supply boats there were many cottagers who managed without any power boat. Today there is at least one motorboat on every one of our 17 islands and on many there are two or more.

Why would anyone want the expense and bother of owning a motorboat during those years when Mr. Kennedy was delivering groceries? I suspect a fear of possible accidents encouraged such ownership. Without telephones or radios to summon help our early cottagers could only rely on a powerboat in an emergency. This fear of accidents increased when parents began to bring their children to the cottage. At any rate, few who were without children bought boats. Some, of course, found other reasons to own a boat, a desire

2:4. Groceries have arrived! C. C. Kennedy's boat at the dock at B 980 in 1930s

for frequent mail delivery or for fresh meat and milk between Kennedy's visits. The post office and the store at the Ojibway provided inducement.

The first boats were usually inboards with two cycle engines started, when and if they started, by the operator's turning the heavy flywheel by hand. The Giovannolis had a beautiful white Richardson Special with a one cylinder engine (fig. 2:5). Leonard used it for an almost daily run to the Ojibway for mail and to purchase meat for his neighbors. Mr. Riley had a one cylinder engine in a lapstrake mahogany boat pointed at both bow and stern. The Donovan clan had a large old green sponson canoe powered by a two cylinder engine whose greater power was cancelled by the difficulty in starting the engine, in keeping it running when once started, and in steering the boat, if by some chance it actually ran. I have

2:5. An early motorboat. The Giovannoli Family in their new Richardson Special in the 1920s.
(l. to r.), Harry, Polly, Aunt Olive, Leonard

a vivid memory of my brother Dick using an oar as a supplement to the tiller in order to negotiate the "S Turn" during a rare trip into Pointe au Baril. This boat had no skeg, so my father was always worried about hitting a rock and, sure enough, once we lost the propeller completely near Carolyn. All these boats were unreliable. One of the miracles of our present age is that all the water and dirt contaminating the gasoline in former years has now disappeared! Most of our trips were interrupted by engine failure; few are today. No longer do water pumps fail, shear pins shear, little children weep and grown men swear. No longer does Mr. Riley, together with a rather large female companion, hike across 500 A after motor failure while coming out Hemlock Channel. And no longer does one hear the endless debates over whether a motor was better located midships which caused exhaust to blow over passengers in the stern or in the stern which caused the operator's view to be obstructed by passengers farther forward! But propellers still hit rocks to be damaged or lost and mechanical problems have not disappeared. However, in our present period we expect our boats to run when we board them and are surprised when they do not. The reverse was once true!

The outboard motor was slow to appear and offered few advantages in reliability at first. The Giovannolis were the first to try one in our area, but after a year or two they exchanged it for an inboard. In the northern area Ethel Williams was the first to own one. When I was a boy, she seemed remarkable in this, too: she was the only woman I knew who operated a motor herself and she had such a powerful one, a Johnson of five horsepower. We ourselves acquired an Evinrude, a more modest two and one half horsepower, in 1937 or 1938. That little motor attached to a flat-bottomed wooden rowing skiff purchased from Eaton's for $75 and named Tobey was our motorboat after the demise of the green sponson. It provided, as did all such motors of the time, the excitement of the erratic starter rope. The flywheel was turned by the use of a rope with a knot in one end fitted into a notch on the wheel and a wooden handle on the other end. When pulled smartly the knotted end frequently snapped back hitting the head of any unwary passenger. If the motor failed to start on the first pull, and it almost always failed, the rope had to be carefully rewound on the flywheel before the second pull. Once started our motor, I recall, often stalled either because the gasoline line had become clogged with dirt or because the water pump failed. But one could always break out oars and row.

Because of the smallness of both our boats and motors a visitor commented once that there was only one proper boat in our community, the four cylinder inboard "Fayola," Dr. Pope's pride and joy. When, as a teenager, I helped the Popes it was a treat to be allowed to take the wheel occasionally and Dr. Pope taught me to use four pine trees on E 19 as a landmark on the return from Turning Rock, a landmark I still use. I was not to operate a boat with a steering wheel again for over twenty years.

After the war the horsepower race was on. My father purchased an air-cooled Lawson motor in 1946. No more water pump failures for this six horsepower beauty! There was one problem: the motor was almost impossible to start. So, by the late 1950s the Lawson was replaced by a conventional Johnson, but now even more powerful. I think its ten horsepower was as much as my father would ever have considered. As an adult I overcame caution and purchased a twenty-five horsepower motor. Today I am amazed that I am using a seventy horsepower motor. Where will it end?

In the early years motorboats were used almost exclusively

for utilitarian purposes, usually for short runs in good weather to the Ojibway. While Leonard made frequent trips, we made, at most, only one a week. We rarely used motorboats for recreation. We never fished from them. We did not water ski (the motors were too small in any event to pull skiers). I remember once we tried to use a shutter as an aquaplane, but it somehow dove into the mud and was lost, putting an end to that activity. Normally the only recreational use of motorboats was for long expeditions. Trips to the McCoys or Limestones, down Frederic Inlet to a picnic spot on Shawanaga, or, very rarely, to the Shawanaga River or to the Lighthouse were best undertaken in a motorboat. Often, because of the large number of us involved, we might tow one or two canoes with their passengers. Such expeditions were, however, exceptional and until 1960 we used the rowboat and canoe for our recreational boating. In them we gathered on Carolyn or on our "Sunset Point" for a communal picnic or at one of the cottages for games. At night no motorboats disturbed the dark waters: we paddled home. Lucy Young paddled for picnics from her island to distant Carolyn. The ladies from Nokomis came to picnics, Peggy Hamilton rowing and Miss Fuller erect in the stern steering with a rope in either hand attached to the tiller's yoke. Our major source of energy was the human body. Perhaps we were healthier as a consequence and the environment less polluted?

To complete our journey to the island by powerboat a dock at which to land and disembark was needed. With rocky shores and changing water levels it has always been difficult to construct and preserve docks. Docks provide another ongoing and unchanging challenge for all cottagers. The simplest solution, no longer in favor, is not to have any dock at all, but to have boats draw alongside the rocky shore wherever it shelves off steeply enough to permit such an approach. For years water taxis landed against the shore on the Groves' island opposite Fayola, although, as I recall, a floating log was tethered there to protect the hulls from the abrasive rock. Not even that protection was provided at E 3 where, despite several attempts, no dock survived along that steep rocky shore (fig. 2:6). Boats thus had to draw up against the rock and passengers climb out. At least once Archie Taylor found himself catching a passenger who fell backwards on that climb! Needless to say, this solution which was no solution was not popular with the operators of the

2:6. Landing without a dock. Archie Taylor's water taxi at E 3 in the late 1940s

taxis and boat ownership itself made it necessary to provide some secure dockage for one's investment.

In the early periods of our story two slightly differing approaches were tried to solve the dock problem. The first and easier was to find a configuration of the rocks along the shore which could support and keep secure log stringers upon which a board decking was constructed. Our island (B 980) was fortunate in this regard as was Mr. Riley's. Dr. Pope managed to construct a successful dock on the front of Fayola despite the fact that the rocks were not really accommodating. His dock survived because it was very small and was strengthened by vertical supports wedged into a crevice. The docks required much labor to build but fortunately were not expensive since logs were there for the taking. Alas, they frequently broke up in the spring under the assaults of melting ice and always washed out when the lake level rose. During the 1930s lumbering came to an end, but many stray logs were still to be found washed up. At the start of each summer one need only paddle around shores and shoals to locate suitable specimens. Then levers, ropes, and rowboats for towing soon brought in logs for a dock. One hazard that made a lasting impression upon me was encountered by my older brothers and cousins as they attempted to retrieve such a

2:7. The original dock on B 980. Bob Donovan and Jim Erdmann on the diving tower; George Erdmann and Dick Donovan on the dock in 1937

log washed into the shallows off the outer shore of Fireplace Island. They all developed a rash after wading around that log and ever afterwards we spoke of "itchitis." I am reluctant to wade there to this day. Boards for decking, too, were reused. Because these docks washed out so often there was frequently salvage to be found at the beginning of each season downwind from a dock's original location. Those boards were fair game for the first to arrive. In the mid 1930s my brother Dick and cousin Jim Erdmann, both still in their teens, built a dock on the front of B 980 (with some help in moving the logs from the younger Bob and George). This was a more elaborate dock with a diving tower at one end supported on posts fashioned from the trunks of a few cedars cut for this purpose (fig. 2:7). On the top of this tower, too young to dive, I used to lie to watch for Mr. Kennedy's boat each week. Because the water level was consistently low in the 1930s this dock survived for years and was later rebuilt more than once, without the tower, in the same location.

2:8. The French boathouse as finished in 1965

Alternatively dock builders sank a crib or cribs filled with rocks to support one end while the other they anchored on shore. These docks required much more labor, more logs, and dock spikes, but they could be built on islands like E 3 where the shore was not suitable for the former type. These docks were usually professionally built. The most elaborate one was that constructed by Steve French behind Sagastaweekee which supported a large boat house with bedrooms on a second floor (fig. 2:8). Its cribs can still be seen underwater. Changing water levels, ice and rot sooner or later destroyed these docks, too.

After the war my father had a new idea, a dock cantilevered out over the water supported by metal girders bolted to the rock. He had such a dock built on the front of B 980, but we quickly discovered two problems. The first was that the location was too exposed: no boat could safely be left there in a strong south wind. The second problem was that, when the water level rose, ice caused the metal girders to bend and snap destroying the wooden decking as well. It was an experiment never to be repeated, although a far more elaborate version is to be found on Carolyn today. In this dock the girders, together with the decking, can be adjusted up or down as water levels change.

Currently we have abandoned, for the most part, the fixed dock and replaced it with the floating dock fixed by chains to anchors at its outer end and to bolts set in the rock on the inner with a ramp to shore. Changing water levels do not destroy these docks, although their location along the shore may have to be shifted. But this solution to the dock problem has brought new difficulties as well. These docks are more costly to construct. They rot like all wooden docks. They have to be protected from beaver and muskrats who find them irresistibly attractive as homesites. They have to be protected in winter by being beached, towed to protective coves, or allowed considerable slack. Finally, professional builders, not cottagers, are usually required to construct a floating dock, to prepare it for the winter, and to reposition it for use the following summer. Will we ever solve the problem of docks?

The acquisition of expensive motorboats created another problem. An owner needed some shelter for the boat to protect the investment. Boathouses like those found north of Carolyn were, with the exception of the one at Sagastaweekee, never built in our group of islands. South of us in Frederic Inlet Mr. Anderson built one as did Mr. Straight. Our boats, however, were so small and inexpensive that a traditional boathouse seemed unnecessary. Ethel Williams' father built a rough shelter for her boat in a cove on the north side of E 18, but there was no dock there, nor a proper boathouse. In the 1960s George Erdmann constructed on E 27 our only permanent boathouse, but it was an usual one. He built it not for a motorboat, but for the sailboat he had constructed, the Gryphon. He built it not on cribs, but on the shore above the high water mark where the sloping rock made it possible to pull a boat up with rollers and mechanical help.

Safely ashore on the island we have completed our journey and are ready to open the cottage. There have been many builders of our cottages over the years beginning with Olver Reid himself. Most of the cottages constructed in the 1930s are the work of Charles Thorkildsen and his large family. All were very simple frame structures to which sooner or later a stone fireplaces and chimneys were usually added. Much later Dudley Curry wrote the following description of "the Georgian Bay Cottage:"

> A cottage in Georgian Bay is nothing like a house. It has no foundations that seat it in deep soil or hard pan clay as a house has. A house is permanently anchored in terra firma, united with the earth like a tree and its roots.

A cottage squats on hard gray or pink rock and just sits there, hopefully clinging there like a barnacle or snail against the sometimes terrible storms of summer and winter.

Some Georgian Bay cottages are on short stumpy legs just high enough to keep the floor out of the rain water or spring runoff. Others are perched on stilt-like pilings made of rock pancakes or, more modernly, on concrete blocks. Older ones just balance on crooked rock legs that don't even have the benefit of mortar. Yet, I've never seen one fallen over because of bad legs. Maybe the magnetic fields of the North Country keep them upright through a mystical gyroscopic power. Maybe, North Country builders have secret techniques.

A house is finished inside with walls of plaster or wall board, and it is even usually insulated in an effort to make it a cozy human nest of even temperatures no matter what the outside is like.

A cottage is unfinished, having its studs and rafters showing in all their nakedness. There is a floor and a roof and sheeted sides—but that's it. Living in a cottage is visually like living inside the skeleton of a big fish. You are surrounded by 2 x 4 ribs on the sides and 2 x 6 (or 8) rafters up above.

After a summer in the cottage, going home to adorned walls, even temperatures and wall-to-wall carpeting is so transforming that even your personality seems to change—frontier person into soft, guilty, comfortable city dweller.

A cottage is attuned to the exterior environmental conditions. The roof may be impermeable and the floor, too, but the siding, even tongue and groove siding, leaks air and some rain water. New siding can be put on really tight, but once the wood begins to dry out and get baked by several seasons of Canadian sunshine, forget it.

In the spring and fall the cottage will be cold. The wind will whisper or whistle through the cracks. The fireplace or the wood stove becomes a hot pocket surrounded by frigid air. You must turn yourself around in front of the fire like you would cook a really tall, standing hot dog—you all the time wearing your outdoor hooded coat.

Outside the wind will whoosh through the pines and cedars in a continuous roar—as though there was a waterfall nearby. This sound does not convey any feeling of warmth.

No one is foolish enough to be in a cottage in the winter. But everyone is foolish enough to be in a cottage in the summer. On a summer morning the cottage will be chilled from the crystal-starred night, but by noon it has become an oven. The breeze that grows with the dawn's rays slowly drops off until the lake world is doubled with its own reflections—a totem morning, we call it because a shoreline looked at sidewise is a natural totem pole design—and the breeze seems slowly swallowed by the stillness and growing heat. The siding and the roof bake and the rock all around sears and it is time to picnic and swim and come back inside when the sun shows signs of letting up.

Of course, each cottage makes its own noises and sounds through the heating and cooling of a day. The cooling sounds are especially noticeable because the cottage activity quiets towards bedtime. Certain boards sound and you know which part of the cottage is doing what as they pop or boom or crack. We have a front porch siding board that snaps out a strong clear signal that all is cooling well.

A cottage has its own light phenomena, also. The cottage on the east side of an island gets the dawn view. The sun is orange as it rises (in case you never saw it) and it can dye a whole bed-room and your hands and curtains and clothes that beautiful color for a few minutes.

The sun yellows as it climbs the wall and then it jumps into the rafters and dances when it strikes the lake and reflects upward into the interior. The cottage principle of the dawn is that sun-light goes down outside and up inside as the sun rises.

Pine siding—and probably spruce, too—has knots a-plenty. When sunlight strikes right through a knot, a round universe of light forms. It glows yellow at the edge and blends through orange to a peculiar near-maroon circle at the center, the color of which can only be called "pine-knot."

Finally, a cottage is empty at least half the year, more like eight or nine months probably. We see it in the warmth of the year. It is hard to imagine it buried in the deep snow and battered by

2:9. The very "basic" cottage built by the Reads on E 27 in 1933

winter storms. It probably makes a whole range of noises we'll never hear. Oh well, it's best to think of the summer season to come.

The challenges of life on our islands are not over upon arrival at the end of our journey. Cottages have to be opened and cottages have to be closed. While details may differ from one person to another and while cottages with simple equipment require different measures from those with more elaborate plants all of us face similar tasks. We have a winter's accumulated dirt to clean out and unpacking to do. At summer's end we pack up once again and dispose of any remaining food. For almost all of us, however, opening begins before we arrive and closing is completed after our departure.

Local contractors have always been hired to put on or remove storm doors and shutters, put up and take down screens, connect and disconnect water pipes, and, in many cottages, remove and put back in those boats stored inside over the winter. Some cottagers have not needed this service, especially if, without water pipes or pumps, they hauled their water in buckets from the lake. The Reads on E 27, for example, had a very basic cottage without sink or pump (fig. 2:9). Its floor was the flat rock upon which the cottage was built. Because there was so little work to do they hired no helpers, although they did store a rowboat and a canoe inside.

Sooner or later every cottager has problems with mice and the attempts to frustrate their destructive habits create many of the chores associated with opening and closing. The challenge is to find ways of protecting mattresses, cushions, etc. from being destroyed by nesting mice over the long winter months. At first my parents suspended a cot frame on wire from the rafters and on this frame all the mattresses were piled. Then mice climbed down the wires and destroyed the bedding. Next from old pie tins and can lids we made "rat guards" for the wires. The mice countered by dropping from the roof onto the suspended bedding. Ethel Williams on E 18 was the first to try lining a closet with wire screening and storing bedding inside. The next step in the escalating war with mice was taken by the Groves who had a large storage box built lined with screening but with open panels on the sides so that it could be used as a bed in the summer. Then a local contractor, John Hodgson, suggested that mice would be unlikely to gnaw their way into a closed and filled wooden box. These mattress boxes, even though unprotected by screening, have been effective. Such radical measures meant, of course, that we have to unload these boxes, air the contents, and reassemble the beds on opening. At closing the morning of departure is even more hectic as we lug every mattress to a box and hoist it in.

In other cottages, where mice infestation was less frequent or less destructive, the owners found easier means of defense. The Erdmanns on E 27, for example, left their sheets and blankets on the beds but covered them securely with heavy plastic well tucked in. The advantages are obvious, but the method has not been entirely effective. Once, on opening night, Sue slid between the sheets to discover that mice were co-tenants at the foot of the bed! On the principle that mice will not invade a cottage filled with light, newcomers are leaving windows unshuttered and everything in place when they depart. This reliance on the deterrent effect of light makes opening and closing easier, but we old timers shake our heads and await the disaster we feel will surely follow before long!

Bedding is not the only home for these pesky rodents. They have built their nests inside the kitchen stove, beneath propane refrigerators, in cutlery drawers in kitchen cabinets, in tool closets, indeed in almost every nook and cranny that cottages provide.

Defensive measures include emptying and overturning all drawers, leaving all closets open, and putting everything possible in the boxes or trunks. When such measures are taken both opening and closing demand many additional hours of work.

Unfortunately mice do not disappear once the cottage is open. However, traps or poison can control their attempts at co-existence. My father, ever the enthusiast for technological innovation, when a fireplace was under construction in our cottage, decided that a newly patented device, the "heatalator," should be installed. A metal plate at the rear with an airspace behind produced additional heat through convection. The heated air passes up from behind the plate and out into the room through a passage in the stones which terminates in a grilled opening in the face of the fireplace. Cold air returns through corresponding grills and passages at the bottom. Mice soon discovered that this network provided a wonderful home beyond the reach of human hands. They sat just inside the grilled openings to watch our frustration and at night they came out to take paper tissue with which to line their nurseries, or to run across occupied beds. Any fire discouraged them for a time and led to a pervasive odor of mouse, but they always returned.

Mice are not the only invaders, nor the only creatures attracted to fireplaces. Ducks seem to be powerfully attracted by chimneys. Many of us, on opening day, have found the huge mess and the breakage of glass and china caused by a panic-stricken duck's attempts to escape from a closed cottage. Often the duck died and the corpse was removed when the contractor arrived to open. Later the owner faced the task of cleaning up the breakage and the "whitewash." Once I recall discovering a duck still flying around inside when we arrived. What a struggle we had to get the stupid bird to fly out the door!

Other creatures may get in, or try to get in, over the summer (recently even bears), but a major pest in our list of those causing problems in closed cottages is that insect we euphemistically call the "pine beetle," although outsiders insist upon calling it a cockroach. These creatures eat some material used in bookbinding, so any hard-covered book that has been on an island bookshelf for some years will show signs of having been attacked. Titles on the spine are obliterated, the letters devoured. These beetles are also fond of crawling over any surface ever touched by food and they leave their spoor on everything. On opening we must thus clean all surfaces in the kitchen, wash all dishes and utensils, and scrub floors. It is such a nuisance to do all that washing before the first meal on arrival that someone was inspired to store dishes and utensils in the plastic bags newly available after the war. We have substituted the labor of bagging and unbagging, both at opening and closing for the washing necessary only at opening. Gladys Dickey and her sister Gwen Erdmann (and perhaps others?) tried the novel idea of rubbing cooking pots with kerosene at the end of the season to discourage both rust and beetles. They even scrubbed floors with kerosene. Again the solution seemed to many of us worse than the original problem. Whatever they cooked in those dishes always had a most distinctive flavour at the beginning of each summer!

No list of pests invading a closed cottage is complete, however, without the inclusion of humans. Fortunately breakins have been relatively uncommon, but when they do occur they are usually destructive—intruders have driven nails through pots and pans, ripped out gas lights, etc. On one memorable occasion in 1982, although they did no damage, the intruders found the island cook book compiled by Aunt Gladys many years earlier. They entered the following account in her book (original spelling and grammar here reproduced):

Our Journal Sept 27, 1982

The 4 of us left from the reaches of Betona. In a 14' wood boat loaded with supplies. After wandering amisely for many hours (2) in the torental rainstorm, with a dead engine we admted defeat and pattled to your lovely abode. Finding the front entrance ajar open however the front room & kitchen insufficient for our needs, we entered the main part our portable heater saved our very lives. We were lost and unable to make camp. We planned to spend the night here. After supper when the whisky was passed around, we found this book. It was a real comfort and we found ourselves enjoying it here and now we are making the best of it and are experiening the pioneer spirit which comes this type of situation. Our recipes would hardly befit such a collection of vocification of culinary egstasy makers. We hope you won't take this the wrong way as we really appreciate your absentee hospitallity which we are sure you would have extended had you been present. As the evening weirs on and the booze wears in, we are getting more content with our shelter. We just did a little fishing. Lost a big pike right at the dock. Getting mellow now listening to Niel Yonge and watching steam leave our wet clothes. The north really does something for you. As we are lost with a broken motor and were having a good time. Tommorow we will shall find the enchanted isle. Our mechanic & ship's captain "Mister Animal Derayal" assures us (the fact that we left on Sun 26th for a 3 hr boat trip shouldn't cause us to disbelieve him. Actually this cabin is much nicer than our's. We desperately appreciate the use of your cabin and if we had any more apropriate means to thank you we would surely do so. Most Sincerely, Rouny, Hen, Pninall, & Gummer

These four then entered their own recipe to add to the others in the book. It is called "Pete's Beef Stew" and calls for 1 can of generic beef stew, 1 can of generic Irish stew, 1 can of Campfire Chile con Carne and 4 oz. of red wine (they recommend "Italian Folinari, or Secco-Bertony, Volpolicia"). They suggest that one "simmer on medium heat on borrowed stove for 18 minutes" and "serve in pots and pans with ladles or serving spoons."

Some less dramatic problems are also becoming less common. I remember the challenge of keeping the prime in the kitchen water pump. Although it was supposed to be in working order when we arrived, it was a rare summer when the pump worked perfectly. No matter what type of pump one had, one had to keep a jug of water handy to prime it before filling a kettle or a wash basin. In those earlier years, too, one could not dash out immediately to use old wooden boats. They had to "soak up." Placed in shallow water they had to sit for a day or two until the wood swelled with the moisture to make the hull, in theory at least, water tight. Today, when hulls are made of fiberglass or aluminum, one forgets the additional yearly tasks of varnishing or painting, scraping, caulking, and patching required for canvas canoes and all wooden boats. While one could pay to have such work done, in our area it was almost always done by the cottagers themselves over the course of the summer.

The trip, arrival and the chores of opening completed one could look forward to the summer ahead. But there were problems in that idyllic time, too. We found it difficult to preserve fresh food and dairy products in kitchens without electricity for refrigerators. In the earliest period cottagers had no means of cooling except those nature provided. They hung fresh produce in baskets from branches of nearby trees. Early on some enterprising souls constructed a box beneath the cottage floor with openings covered by screening for ventilation. Food placed in such a box remained a little cooler. I believe the Giovannoli family on B 945 introduced this method of cooling. On E 3 there is still such a box reached through a trap door in the porch floor. Gladys Dickey, I remember, placed custard cups there filled with gelatin flavored with orange or lemon juice. The boxes worked, at least to produce one of my favorite desserts!

A more effective way to keep food cold was to use ice. In the 1930s we could purchase blocks of ice at the Ojibway for a penny a pound. This ice was cut during the winter from Ojibway Bay and was preserved in sawdust in the ice house on the hotel dock near the present store. Most cottagers had iceboxes and every week went to the Ojibway, bought a block of ice and brought it back in a tub or, in our family, in a galvanized metal baby bathtub. In our cottage we have the ice tongs and ice pick from that era. It was a great moment when the ice was hauled up to the cottage, the block chipped to fit, and slipped into place. Those chips made it possible for us to make iced lemonade or tea on that one day each week. One year some stomach upsets gave rise to suspicions about the purity of the water from which the ice was formed. These blocks of ice did not last more than a few days, especially during hot weather, so we rushed to enjoy fresh meat and fresh milk on our cereal. When the fresh milk, in glass bottles from the Georgian Bay Creamery, ran out or soured, the only substitute was an early form of powdered milk sold under the trade name, Klim (milk spelled backwards). Klim was powdered whole milk which required prodigious stirring with an egg beater before it would dissolve and when it did, the resulting liquid tasted terrible. "Chalky" was our descriptive term for it. This milk substitute was satisfactory in cooking and the large Klim cans had many uses. Definitely it was not for drinking! Perhaps for that reason we all became tea drinkers at an early age and tea remains the usual beverage we offer to our guests.

This use of ice for refrigeration explains the pattern of the week's gastronomy before the war. We ate fresh meat and vegetables for a few days after supplies came in and the ice held. After that we switched to tinned foods, baked beans, corned beef hash, etc. and cabbage slaw, in our house made with a bit of canned pineapple, for salad. Melt water drained through a pipe to exit at the bottom of the icebox. There was always talk of drilling a hole in the floor beneath for this water and perhaps in some cottages this was done. In ours it was always just talk, so we had to keep a pan under the icebox which, if the child whose responsibility it was to empty it forgot, would overflow across the floor as a reminder. The most unusual icebox was in the cottage on Fayola, not a proper box at all but an old trunk.

There was one cottage in the 1930s were ice was not used for refrigeration. On Chinook, E 18, Ethel Williams had a marvel, a true refrigerator whose trade name was the "Icy Ball." It was the envy of the Bay, although my family made disparaging comments about the nuisance of having to heat the "ball" each day on its separate little burner before the ball mechanism was dropped back into the chest to do its cooling work.

All this changed during the time of transition after the war. By 1955 our cottage had a proper fridge, an old Servel, fueled by propane. These same refrigerators could be fueled alternately with kerosene, so, in either configuration, they could be used in islands without electricity and all cottagers soon had them. Proper refrigeration changed our way of life forever. With careful planning the intervals between shopping trips could now be extended from days to weeks. Diets, too, changed. Other salads frequently replaced slaw. Cold milk was no longer a rare treat. But those early gas refrigerators did not have true freezers making the storage of frozen food and ice cream impossible. Gradually that reassuring sight in the old cottage kitchen, a wall of shelves holding tinned meats, vegetables, and fruit, disappeared. Many a taste from childhood for me is now but a memory. No longer do we require the teenage appetites to finish off every morsel at a meal because now we can keep leftovers. Still I expect there are those, like my brother Dick, known in the family as "seagull" for his ability to finish off everything, who will remind us

2:10. Island appetites. Jim Erdmann, Dix McDonald,
Dick Donovan at a community picnic on E 5 in the mid 1930s

that island appetites are prodigious (fig. 2:10). From the time of the earliest cottagers the claim has been made that food tastes better here. It is a claim verified anew by the experience of each generation. Gladys Dickey, in the preamble to her "Island Cookbook," described our appetites:

> Thank heaven our four teen-agers had lusty appetites, although the voids to be filled were sometimes slightly terrifying. There was very little they wouldn't eat (one time they made lichen soup) and at lightening speed, too. George (Erdmann) holds a record of ten pieces of french toast consumed in twelve minutes according to Helen Addington's watch (a guest that summer). One time I was about to throw away some fudge squares I had thriftily made with bacon grease. It was the middle of the morning when the boys landed from a two or three day canoe trip to the French River. In a trice they had gulped down all the fudge squares and survived!

In a similar vein Bob Donovan speaks of Hope's encounter with island appetites on her first visit to our shores:

In those distant unliberated days, the cooking fell exclusively to the women, who each took a day in turn to prepare all the meals. Hope had difficulty in coming to terms with island appetites and could never quite manage to prepare more food than the family could dispose of at one sitting. She made a stew in the dutch oven, and she insists that she actually mounded it up in the dome lid, but to no avail. It was all devoured, and half an hour later teen-age boys would be making themselves peanut butter sandwiches in the kitchen.

Propane not only changed our lives through refrigeration but also, although less dramatically, through cooking. In earlier times most cottagers used the three-burner kerosene stove. However, Mr. Riley used an old wood burning range in his kitchen upon which, I was told, once a summer he cooked a wonderful repast to which he invited only the women in the Bay. After lunch he asked them to clean up and they discovered that he had dirtied practically every pot he owned. They also encountered the major drawback to the wood range in summer—heat in the kitchen! Many of us have written of the kerosene stoves used for so many years. Bob Donovan adds this contribution to the lore:

My younger readers, nurtured on propane stoves equipped with pilot lights, can have no real conception of the difficulties of preparing a dinner on a three-burner kerosene stove. Bear in mind that my father did not consider anything less than a roast, with potatoes, gravy, hot vegetable, salad, dessert, and coffee worth sitting down to on a Sunday. Not for him the simple casserole that "needs only a green salad and a crusty french loaf to make a satisfyingly complete meal" (in the language of modern cookbooks). Remember, too, that the oven was a cumbersome chest that had to be retrieved from its usual place under the sink and lifted onto the stove, where it took up two burners, leaving only one for everything that had to be cooked on top of the stove.

The ritual began by turning the knob of the burner six complete turns to the left. This released a flow of kerosene to the asbestos ring at the heart of the burner. After several minutes

2:11. Didge Donovan cleaning the tempermental kerosene stove

the ring became saturated and could be lit with a match, and then the handle had to be turned completely off while the flickering flame crept around the ring. Then the handle was turned on again, a scant half turn, and the burner began to produce (in theory, at least) a steady blue flame, hot enough to boil water in a matter of twenty minutes or so. If the pot boiled over (as it sometimes did), of course the burner was "chilled" and out of service for that meal, unless everything came to a halt while the stove was dismantled out on the rock and a new asbestos ring installed (fig 2:11). With luck, however (and ceaseless vigilance), such disasters could be avoided. Imagine, then, the pie now cooling on a rack, and the roast, surrounded by potatoes, sputtering in the oven, the vegetables simmering in a double boiler (of which both parts were frequently in use at once) on the odd burner. Suddenly the burners begin to fail, and it is discovered that the glass container at the end of the stove has run out of kerosene. Someone will have to rush it out back to the kerosene drum, refill it, and rush it back to the stove before all the burners go out. You can't get the container back in place without spilling some kerosene, and of course you get some on your hands. You can never quite get rid of the smell, and the whole meal finally comes to the table redolent of kerosene. You get the idea.

These stoves sometimes presented still more challenges: water might contaminate the kerosene requiring the entire system to be drained; sometimes dirt clogged the narrow pipes preventing the kerosene from reaching the burners. We became adept at coping with such emergencies. The ovens, too, could not be regulated and asbestos pads were inserted above the burners to retard the heat and boards placed on top to encourage even browning. What amazes me today is that so many wonderful dinners, so much baking, emerged from those early kitchens. Gladys Dickey comments:

> I've found an almost irresistible desire to bake on a rainy day. How delightful it is to have cookies ready if some neighbors have braved the wind and the rain to pay you a visit.
>
> And on the other hand, when you've spent much time and long hours in that miserable little kitchen with that wretched stove, and you're absolutely fed up, don't despair! Make your escape! Take to the canoe, and when you are afloat and moving, everything falls into its proper place, and a heavenly peace descends upon you.
>
> Before I end I must add a word in praise of kerosene. Dip a wad of toilet paper in it to clean the stove, and the sink. Use it to mop up the floors once in a while. Helen (Whitelaw) has even used it on her hair just before she washed it. But I wouldn't recommend that. However, I'm sure there are many more things it can be used for. One of the most useful "aids" to housekeeping on the island...I have also found it gives out quite a good deal of heat, when you pull your stove into that large, lofty living room on an August morning when the thermometer is in the forties. It is also a deterrent for roving roaches when it is put in coffee cans in which table legs rest...

Propane for cooking brought an end to the problems of the kerosene stove. The major change in cooking made possible by this new fuel was in baking. The new propane stoves had proper ovens whose heat could, theoretically, be regulated automatically by the turn of a dial. I say theoretically because so many of these stoves had faulty regulators and bakers had to learn to monitor the heat constantly as it usually either rose rapidly, or fell suddenly. Maintaining a steady temperature was virtually impossible. Perhaps baking in an

2:12. The "kitchen" of the Reads outside their cottage on E 27

island kitchen will always end in a race to produce a product baked above before it is burned below!

Some cooking has always been done outside the cottage. Of course, picnics frequently required building temporary fireplaces out of loose rocks and using the ever present dead branches of pine for fuel. On E 27 the Reads, however, transformed almost all meals into picnics by constructing a more permanent outdoor fireplace just north of their cottage (fig. 2:12). Here they cooked most of their meals during a summer's stay. My mother liked the idea of cooking some things outside the heat of the cottage kitchen, but objected to the Read's fireplace built so low that the cook had to squat or bend down. My father, uncle, and older brothers, therefore, constructed a permanent stone fireplace just north of our cottage in 1934. It was high enough that one could stand to cook and it had a chimney to carry the smoke away. In practice, however, this fireplace was seldom used for its intended purpose. It was used occasionally for picnics, especially when fish were to be fried or waffles cooked. Waffle picnics had become very popular in the 1920s and remained so through the 1930s, although they are unknown now. The waffle irons, of cast iron, were heated on one side and then swiveled to heat the other. Every time they were turned some batter fell into the fire below but it required no clean up afterwards if that fire was in an open fireplace rather than in the burner of a stove! A fireplace like that on B 980 was constructed by my brother Dick and cousin Jim

2:13. The outdoor fireplace. Dick Donovan and Jim Erdman building one on E 5 1930s

Erdmann, on E 5 (fig. 2:13) and then, reverting to the lower profile, one on Fayola built by brother Bob and cousin George.

Perhaps we should not leave the subject of cooking without including a favorite recipe (slightly modified) from the cookbook Aunt Gladys put together. The advantage of the following recipe is that a blueberry upside down cake takes only half as many berries and thus can be made when the pickers have not managed to come up with the four or five plus cups of blueberries a pie requires.

Blueberry Upside Down Cake

Cook gently for 5 minutes in an uncovered saucepan: 2 cups of blueberries, 1/3 cup sugar, a little lemon juice. Cool. Cream 1/4 cup butter or shortening, 1/2 cup sugar, 1 egg, 1 teaspoon vanilla. Sift dry ingredients 1 1/2 cups of flour, 1 1/2 teaspoons baking powder, 1/4 teaspoon salt. Alternately add the dry ingredients and 1/2 cup of milk to the creamed batter. Beat until smooth. Pour over blueberries in greased and floured 8 x 8 pan. Bake at 350 for approximately 25 minutes. Allow to cool for ten minutes before inverting to turn out with blueberry layer on top.

Another change propane brought, although less important than in refrigeration and cooking, was in lighting. Without electricity we had to make do with the dim light of kerosene lamps. Even the brightest of them, the "Aladdins," used mantles subject to flaming. Whenever flames engulfed the mantle the light had to be turned very low until the soot burned off. A few tried lanterns, but the storage of still another type of fuel, white gas, and their hiss when in use limited their popularity. My uncle, Morris Erdmann, sought a brighter light by using the British made "Tilley" lamp. This burned kerosene, but produced the same hissing as the lantern. With propane came propane lights and almost every cottage soon had one or more. For the first time it became possible to wash dishes after dark in a kitchen where there was enough light to see what had been left on the plates! Games and parties could now continue into the night with better illumination. Most reading, however, was still done by the light of the kerosene lamp perched beside chair or bed where it had to be shielded from the drafts lest the flame flicker and the glass chimney become blackened by soot.

All these changes have made life easier and more convenient, but they have also exacted a price: we have become more dependent upon outside help, upon resources back on the mainland. Before the war, cottagers were far more self-reliant, requiring the help of a contractor only for opening and closing. We made do with amateur repairs, seeking the help of Albert Demasdon at the Ojibway to repair a motor when our own efforts failed. We shopped at the Ojibway where clerks behind the open counters facing the dock filled our orders and, in a little shop behind, the butcher cut our meat (fig. 2:14). Down the dock we stopped for ice and gasoline. Laundry we did by hand in tubs, rinsing in the lake. In our cottage each child was responsible for doing his or her own laundry. For a few years at closing we could take our sheets to the laundry at the Ojibway to be picked up clean the next summer. Even mail could be sent and received at a seasonal post office at the Ojibway. In more

2:14. The store on the dock at the Ojibway Hotel in the 1920s

recent decades, however, we shop in the supermarkets in Parry Sound as well as in Kennedy's and the Ojibway store. We go to the post office in Pointe au Baril and we wash our laundry at the laundromat in Parry Sound. Before we hauled our own ice and kerosene but today we depend upon a contractor to deliver a big tank of propane every few weeks. At the beginning of each season we must have a professional clean the flue and trim the flame of the refrigerator. That feeling that we were on remote islands cut off from civilization fades before the greater dependence on modern technology. Today the radio telephone and the cell phone keep us in touch at all times both with each other and those at a distance. The early cottagers, however, came here in part to avoid the telephone and its distractions! Yet there is a positive side to these developments as well: island life is now possible for those whom old age or infirmity once kept away and it is now safer for everyone. The season, too, has now been extended; we can come and go from spring into the fall, no longer entirely dependent on the Ojibway, open only in July and August.

The years have witnessed the gradual closing of the gap

between life at "home" and life at the "island." Still in our little group our greater isolation preserves some of the differences, not only from life in the city, but also from life on islands north of Carolyn. We still do not have electricity, although it has reached Carolyn itself. Not one of us has a septic field and flush toilets. There are no gasoline powered water pumps and pressurized water systems which duplicate the running water found in city houses. These amenities were not found in our islands in earlier years; now solar power for electric water pumps and propane for hot water heaters are making change possible. But even before the war such systems were common north of Hemlock Channel and were even found in Frederic Inlet south of our group. I remember being so impressed on a visit with my aunt, Gladys Dickey to the cottage on B 867. It not only had a huge boathouse but a water tank on a tower behind the cottage. The owner used a hand pump to fill the tank making possible running water for a bathroom fitted with a wood-fired hot water heater and a claw-footed bathtub! But, whenever water was brought into a cottage its disposal presented a problem not encountered back in the city. In our cottages our pumps emptied into sinks set in wooden counters. Those sinks drained directly out depositing the "gray water" into bushes at some distance from the shore; if the cottage was close to the shore that waste water was likely to drain all too swiftly back into the lake.

In the early days our grey water came from kitchen sinks, not from our bathing. The contents of our morning wash basin we dumped in the nearest bush and for baths we plunged into the lake. Betsy Read Holt remembers that her family bathed on one side of their island and drew their water for drinking from the opposite side! We bathed in tubs only when quite small (fig. 2:15) or, in my family, on the night before departing at the end of the season. Then buckets of water were heated on the stove and in the steamy kitchen, in the glow from the kerosene lamp, we bathed in the old galvanized baby bathtub. Much of that water splashed on the floor as I tried to get more of me into a tub designed for infants! My mother insisted on this one hot bath a summer before we put on the dress clothes so carefully pressed with irons heated on the stove and rubbed over cedar boughs for the trip home. She believed one should be clean and properly dressed for travel.

2:15. The "hot" bath: Sean and Bridget Donovan share the tub, 1990s

Talk of plumbing always leads to a discussion of perhaps the greatest problem in the our occupation of islands like these, the disposal of human waste. Over the years we have been saying to one another that no conversation between cottagers can end without some discussion of our toilets and I here offer another example of this truism! In the earliest days when there were so few visitors and they came for such short periods the most rudimentary privies were adequate, although never pleasant. On islands with great gullys or ravines such privies were similar to the deep pit toilets dug in soft soil throughout rural North America, but for those of us on flat rocks our outhouses required wooden boxes in lieu of the pit. We had to remove these boxes and dump their contents periodically, always the most unpleasant task each summer! Our outhouse had a box beneath, a bench seat with two holes above, each fitted with a circular wooden lid. After each use we were supposed to sprinkle chloride of lime into the box and I remember shaking the cardboard cylinder in which this product was sold while trying to jump out the door before being dusted and choked by the rising cloud of white particles.

Instead of the traditional privy other cottagers used the chemical toilet. This toilet, too, was usually put in an outhouse some distance from the main cottage and consisted of a large galvanized bucket containing the chemical. I do not know the composition of the chemical supplied by the manufacturer of these toilets; I do know that a mixture of lye and water was commonly used as a replacement. The lye caused the container to rust through after a few years. This bucket was placed inside an outer metal can with a civilized toilet seat and lid. The advantage was a toilet similar to those in the city and with less odor than the box privy, but this toilet had to be emptied more frequently. Gladys Dickey said that she had to dump hers every third day or the bucket became too heavy for her to lift. Clearly for both types of toilet there was the problem of where to dump. No place on these islands was truly so far from the lake that one could be confident that there would be no polluting drainage. And it was from those same waters of Georgian Bay that we all took, untreated, our drinking water. Still, in those early summers we assumed that the paucity in our numbers, the limited periods of occupation, and our remoteness from the more intensively occupied islands between the Ojibway and Pointe au Baril would keep our water forever pure and clear. These past decades have seen that misguided confidence destroyed.

The first change made in our sanitary systems probably made matters worse. In the 1950s, at the same time that cottagers discovered propane, they discovered septic tanks. But the tanks we installed were never connected to septic fields. Rather, as was true of "grey water" from kitchen sinks, the flow from these tanks was discharged into bushes and rocks adjacent to the outhouse or cottage. The toilet was placed directly above the tank, or at a short distance from it, and flushed with a small amount of water after each use. No longer was it necessary to dump, but the former chore was replaced by carrying, or pumping, water to the toilet. There was still labor but it was not dirty and unpleasant. Problems with this new system quickly appeared. The tanks rusted through after a few years and had to be replaced leaving a graveyard of old tanks rusting away in the thickets. On some islands too large a number of residents from time to time overwhelmed the capacity of the tank leading to rapid run off into Georgian Bay. In the end this use of tanks was banned.

Currently there are three approved methods to solve this problem of human waste: the holding tank pumped out regularly, a full septic field, and a composting toilet. Our cottagers favor this third solution, the composting toilet. No one in our community has a holding tank or septic field, although they can be found as near as Carolyn to the north and Frederic Inlet to the south. At this date it does not appear likely that there will ever be a completely satisfactory solution. These islands are not suited for the disposal of human wastes of whatever sort and the increase in our number makes matters worse. I expect that every island conversation will continue to include some mention of our PROBLEM!

Despite all these changes over the years most of the cottages on our seventeen islands continue to be what our good local realtor, Neil Cameron, classifies as "basic." In this respect our region continues to differ from others north and south, but the gap is beginning to close as more modern cottages begin to replace older ones. Certainly one may expect that the pattern of the future will mirror our history with more ways to make life easier and more comfortable. But whatever happens I doubt very much that there will be any change in the pleasure our islanders have always taken in their summers "on the Bay!"

The members of our community describe these pleasures in their contributions to this history but I shall provide a brief summary at the outset. Those who have never visited our islands frequently ask us, "What do you do there?" I suspect we cottagers find this a very strange question because our summers never seem long enough for all the things we like, and want, to do.

There are all the things we enjoy doing by ourselves. Reading is certainly high on the list. Books line the walls of many cottages and lending books to one another is a habit. Some who have the talent take pleasure in arts and crafts—Gwen and Sue Erdmann come to mind as do Brownie Baker and Pete McDonald. Some pursue a particular interest in botany or zoology and here one thinks of Margaret and Reid Wilson and their interest in birds, an interest shared by Didge Donovan, of Dix McDonald and Leonard Giovannoli, of Patricia Donovan and Linda McDonald and their interest in wildflowers, and of Dudley and Fran Curry our resident mycologists. In every generation there are individuals eager to fish.

2:16, 2:17, 2:18, 2:19. The Big One! Dix holding his catch, as big as I was (George Erdmann next to me) in the mid 1930s; BELOW Pete McDonald and catch in 1940; Reid Wilson with his, late 1950s; Kevin Donovan holding his catch in 1969

2:20. A community outting to the Limestones in George Erdmann's Gryphon in the late 1960s

Someone in every family has caught at least one "big one" and the struggle to land such a fish is the subject of many stories. One of the first was the pike longer than I was tall that Dix McDonald caught near Riley's Rock in the mid 30s. The whole community gathered to admire his catch (figs. 2:16, 2:17, 2:18, 2:19).

Boating in all its forms is another pleasure either as an activity enjoyed alone or with others. We always associate George Erdmann with sailing, but rowing canoeing and motorboating also have their enthusiasts. Boating, too, leads to exploration, another pleasure. Canoes and rowboats enable us to explore inner channels, quiet bays, and even ponds and swamps found on Big Island or 500 A, while boats powered by wind or engine carry us out to the open bay, the outer islands, the McCoys and Limestones (fig. 2:20), and to other regions farther away.

Picking blueberries and beachcombing are two other activities to be enjoyed by oneself or with a partner. How my father loved both pursuits! Many pleasant hours can be spent walking over the outer shoals to see what treasures the winter storms have tossed up. Twice, while exploring the shoals, I have had the added excitement of finding bottles containing a message.

To solitary pleasures we add the social ones. Swimming, enjoyed by some on their own (Carrie Bartow or Steve Hofmann come to mind), seems even more fun with others. When I was small it was customary for our community to gather at one island or another for a morning or an afternoon swim (around 11 for the former, 3 for the latter). This informal coming together was later expanded into "the swimming party." This means invitations, tea and baked goodies during the afternoon. Indeed the pleasures of table and conversation have been known to lead to some swimming parties in which there was no swimming at all!

In the 1930s the young people who gathered to swim off Chinook frequently went on to a game of Monopoly. Board games, and card games were popular. Scavenger hunts and treasure hunts stand out in our memories, perhaps in part because they did not occur very often. I remember being impressed as a small boy by the ingenuity of those on a scavenger hunt who, among other things, had to find a stick of chewing gum. Unable to find the manufactured sort, they scraped together some pine sap and tried to pass it off as the authentic article by wrapping it in foil! For some reason we began to play charades first after the war and they quickly became popular. Another recent development is the more frequent gathering in the evening for these pastimes, thanks to gas lights.

In earlier times nocturnal social activity took place primarily around a bonfire on a shoal or on the windward shore of an outer island. Drift wood provided fuel, marshmallows and cocoa refreshment, and ghost stories or songs the entertainment. On one occasion on a shoal off E 19 Ernie Pope saw a light from a similar event taking place on Carolyn. Using a flashlight he signaled to those revelers in morse code, "Don't come over. We have no clothes on!" The reply came back at once and flashes of light spelled out this message, "Don't worry. We won't!"

It has been a great blessing that music has been, and seems to continue to be, of the live, not recorded variety. Without mainland electricity radios and record players were largely unknown prior to the war. Jim Erdmann once had a wind-up portable record player and some "78" records that he planned on taking in a canoe of an evening when a young lady might be on board. But, the silence and tranquility of our evenings have rarely been broken by anything but

2:21. The community picnic: gathered outside the cottage on B 980
in the mid 1930s,   (l. to r.), Reuben, Betsy, Eleanor Read
(the names of the other three to the right not recorded)

the call of the loons. To the singing around the bonfires there is the
occasional instrumental accompaniment and our communal musical
evenings, now called hootenannies, are sometimes taking place
indoors.

These nocturnal social activities have been popular with
younger people as their elders are less enthusiastic about paddling
through channels and bays in the dark. The one social event, in addition to the swimming party, that brought all generations together
either at noon or in late afternoon has been the picnic (fig. 2:21). Of
old, each family would bring its food, sometimes with something to
share, and our entire community would gather. A main dish might
be provided by the host family and often this would be fish. Either a
big pike had been caught and ended up in a fish chowder or someone like Morris Erdmann had been very lucky and had enough bass
to fry for everyone. Once I helped him and discovered he had invited everyone before he had the fish in hand. When the bass refused
to cooperate we were reduced to supplementing with rock bass easily caught under any dock. What a chore it was to clean all those

small fish before they were fried on the outdoor fireplace on E 5! Another culinary focus of distant memory now was waffles, as I have mentioned. Several families had waffle irons and at a picnic all were in constant use to produce waffles for the hungry guests. Leonard Giovannoli was particularly fond of this viand! Carolyn Island was the favorite venue for community picnics in those days. The other popular spots were E 5 and either of two places on the outer end of B 980, the one called Sunset Point and the second, slightly more sheltered, called the Inner Point.

Gradually these communal picnics are becoming less common. Today the patterns of urban and suburban social life seem to be taking the place of the picnic. Individual families come together for "sit down" meals in a cottage, often for dinner, arriving and departing (after dark) in power boats. This social activity is no longer confined within the families on our seventeen islands or with those in the adjacent Frederic Inlet. We may now find ourselves as guests of, or hosts to, those whose cottages are anywhere in the Pointe au Baril region. Our horizons are expanding, but perhaps at some cost to our sense of community. Still any threat, be it from fire, accident, or wildlife, brings everyone to rally for the common good and revives those bonds.

There are aspects of life here more important than our recreational pastimes. I think we all discover that we maintain, and may even strengthen, our ties to one another and to our extended families during our summers on Georgian Bay. Members of my family are now scattered widely and we would seldom see each other if we did not meet at our one common home, the island. Friendships, too, grow deeper. Our busy lives during the rest of the year limit our opportunities to enjoy the company and conversation of friends. Here we have time for each other and, for some of us, these island friendships extend over so many years. We have known each other since childhood. We share this history. The focus provided by a small community and summer's leisure enrich our relationships.

I have saved the discussion of perhaps our most wonderful pastime to the last—we enjoy the freedom to do nothing! We are surprised each visit to rediscover the value of unscheduled time. Coming from busy winter schedules we find it difficult at first to relax, but soon we begin to enjoy those times when we simply watch this wonderful world around us and go in thought wherever our minds may take us. Gladys Dickey noted on her map of 1926 a spot on the outer shore of E 19, "Sunny rocks to dream the long hours through." How we all come to appreciate those precious hours!

On a sunny rock. Gladys Dickey on an early visit.

3:22. A Massasauga Rattlesnake snared by Kevin Donovan in 1988

CHAPTER THREE

Rattlesnakes and Bears

No account of our summers would be complete without some discussion of the two forms of wildlife that we have come to find threatening—rattlesnakes and bears. Other animals and insects are either a nuisance or a treasure and some have been discussed above, but the Massasauga rattlesnake and the black bear belong in a separate category as it is almost impossible to share our islands with either and retain any peace of mind. The latter has only recently become a problem in our islands so far from the mainland. Perhaps their number is increasing and their habitat there more threatened. Whatever the reason they are now with us swimming from island to island in search of food. Rattlesnakes, however, have been with us from the start. Officially their numbers are down and they are listed as an endangered species. On our islands their numbers seem far from diminishing and, if not increasing, at least appear to be holding steady.

I myself never saw a rattlesnake during the summers I spent

here as a boy and young man. There was talk of them and I remember walking across E 19 with Pete McDonald when we were 8 or 9 and being told by Pete what I was to do in the event he was bitten. He told me to make transverse cuts with my knife across the puncture wounds left by the snake's fangs and then to suck the venom out. I was far more worried about the prospect of having to treat Pete than of being bitten myself! It was not until I was married that I actually saw my first rattlesnake. Patricia, whom I had told not to worry about these snakes because I had never seen one, found one almost on her first visit and has been finding them ever since. Indeed, for several summers in the 1980s we encountered one every summer just outside our cottage. One year, using an invention devised by David Whitman, a rope noose attached to a long stick, our son Kevin proved that it worked by snaring a rattler right behind our cottage (fig. 3:22). We transported it to another island and discovered a minor flaw in the device—it was easy to draw the noose tight, but it was very difficult to get it to open sufficiently for the snake to escape when we got it to its new home! With great effort, we managed to set it loose.

Islanders have, however, been reporting rattlesnakes from the beginning. The following excerpt from a talk I gave to the Islanders' Association (July 18, 1999) provides a noteworthy example:

> (Leonard Giovannoli) records that in late August, 1924, he captured a live female snake. For the full story, however, one has to turn to a clipping from a newspaper found in his photo album. The headline shrieks "TEN BABY SNAKES." Below that is a subhead, "Born to Rattler Mother at North Ashland Avenue Home— College Student Brings Reptile to Professor." Here is the full text of the article which follows: "Leonard Giovannoli, 162 North Ashland Avenue, brought home with him from his summer wanderings a live rattlesnake, about 28 inches long and carrying seven rattles. This snake he proposed to give to his preceptor, W. D. Funkhouser, head of the department of zoology, University of Kentucky. Leonard was guarding the snake carefully in his bedroom at home and was somewhat surprised Sunday afternoon, upon inspecting the box, to discover that, instead of one rattler, there were eleven in the party, the old snake during the day having multiplied herself to that extent. The 10 young rat-

tlers apparently came into the world panoplied for business since they readily coiled themselves and prepared to "strike," in true snakely manner, at the approach of strangers."

The newspaper seem to have taken some liberties in telling the story for, in Leonard's notes, he records only eight young. A more recent account of our problems with these snakes is provided by Jean Hofmann:

> One summer during the early 1960s, while the Franklin family was staying at Chinook (E 18), our middle sister and her husband, Helen and James Eichert, brought their two young children to visit our parents at Kingbird (E 5).
>
> My sisters, each with small children in tow, set out to find enough blueberries for a pie. They were working on a berry patch in the middle of E 5 when they suddenly became aware of the presence of rattlesnakes in the berry bushes. At the same dreadful moment, they realized that the children were on one side of the patch and the adults on the opposite side.
>
> The frightened mamas were able to persuade the youngsters to stand still until the adults could get to them and move them to safety, but the experience was so unnerving for "Tiny" and Jim Eichert that they never came back to Georgian Bay after that summer.
>
> And although Massasauga rattlesnakes are not a major problem in the area, I do find it a bit disturbing that a majority of the sightings I have heard about over the years have been on Kingbird.
>
> One such sighting occurred in the late 1980s when our son Steve was opening our cottage for the summer and encountered a rattlesnake on the kitchen stove. Steve backed out the door and returned a couple of hours later to an uninhabited stovetop. (I spent a distinctly uneasy summer wondering just how far away that snake had gone.)
>
> In 1993, I was somewhat taken aback to discover a snake, rattling menacingly, just a step or two behind me as I hurried along a path through a low part of Kingbird. I was alone on the island. The snake was between me and the cottage, on a narrow path with swamp on one side and underbrush on the other.

The only sensible course of action seemed to be to wait until it crawled away. More than an hour later, the snake and I still holding one another hostage, my good husband returned and rescued me.

This encounter has disproved my long-held belief that the Massasauga is a timid little snake that will quickly slither away from an approaching human.

And I'm finding it increasingly difficult to take much solace in the other claim I've frequently heard—that the bite of the Massasauga is risky only to young children and to the elderly. My precious grandbabies fall into the first category, and my dear spouse and I are rapidly approaching the other.

While the rattlesnakes have been relatively frequent visitors or occupants on our islands for many years, black bears were not. To be sure, I had been terrified as a child of four at having to go to bed in our bunk house because I was convinced that bears lurked in the thickets just behind the cottage. But I came to realize these feared bears were illusory. Still we were told by Stan Hodgson many years ago that he had seen a bear on our island. Then on walks on Big Island during the 1980s we began to notice signs that perhaps bears were around. It was not until the early 1990s that we actually saw one, however. It was ambling along the shore making its way from E 19 to 500 A. On seeing us it rushed off and we congratulated ourselves on yet another sign of the wild nature of our area. What transformed the bear from treasured wildlife into a threatening menace we now realize began with a well-intentioned effort to be more environmentally responsible.

About this time the Township of the Archipelago in Parry Sound made bins for composting garbage available to all cottagers and these bins seemed to offer a perfect solution to the disposal of kitchen waste. We were warned not to put fat or meat residue in them and, I think, most of us were conscientious in observing these restrictions. What no one seemed to realize was that the aroma emanating from composting garbage drew the bears towards our cottages. Bears probably associated that smell with the potential source of food they had encountered at the town dump south of Pointe au Baril. The events early in the summer of 1995 brought home to us just how serious was our mistake. My log (edited) preserves the record of those dreadful few days:

Wednesday, June 21: The longest day of the year. Patricia and I paddled to a shoal out in the open bay to share a bottle of mead brewed by our son-in-law, David, and to watch the sun go down. A warm evening with only a slight breeze. On our return about 9:30 we heard a thump as we landed the canoe at the front of our island. I carried the paddles up to the storage shed attached to the side of the cottage and found items from it scattered on the ground outside. Patricia went around behind the cottage from the other side and found an empty container of honey on the ground outside the patio door as well as our 2 lb. tub of peanut butter torn open and empty. Sure enough, the screen door, all that was closed between the rock and our cottage, had been ripped from top to bottom. We knew at once we had been invaded by a bear! The first time this had ever happened to me in some 64 years of summering here. What a mess greeted us inside the cottage! Claw marks in the table, holes made by a claw which penetrated more than 40 pages into a new book on Oxford that Patricia had given me, dirty marks on every chair, entire containers of margarine and breakfast cereal emptied, their contents devoured, a tin of marmelade punctured by claws, etc.

We were not allowed to survey the damage for long since the beast, a black bear, suddenly appeared on the path at the rear of the patio. He watched us until I shouted at him at which point he ambled off only to reappear a few moments later. That set the tone for the entire night which followed. Unwilling to sleep on the unprotected screen porch, I brought my mattress inside and tried to sleep on the floor. Every few hours or so, however, the bear came back and tried to gain entry. Patricia kept a pot and spoon by her bed which she sounded when we heard the bear approach. This caused him to withdraw for a bit.

Thursday, June 22: At 4 a.m. the bear tried to tear open the screen on the front porch and around 5 he managed to tear holes in the screen in the front porch door before we could get out there to shoo him away. There was no point in even trying to go back to sleep. We waited in our pajamas for my cousin, George Erdmann, to pass by on his morning constitutional row. Sure enough, at 6:20 he hove into view and we hailed him. He reported that he had seen a bear outside their cottage at supper time the night before. (E 27 is about three fourths of a mile NE of ours.) It probably was the same bear who then swam from island to island over to us. At 7 we turned on our radio telephone and contacted people on the mainland. Word came back shortly from the Ministry of Natural Resources that, although they live trap nuisance bears and move them to new locations, their steel traps are too large and heavy to get onto a boat. Such bears on islands must, therefore, be shot and the owners of property are authorized to shoot them on their own land. No one is prepared, however, to come out to shoot our bear unless we know exactly where he is and we only know that when he is literally at the door! What a feeling of frustration!

Telephoned to other islanders near us. Karin French (cottage about a half mile S across the bay) reported that a bear was on her wooden deck during the morning—ours, or another? Another neighbor, Pete McDonald came over with his dog to see if our bear could be tracked. The dog was totally uninterested, but we did see many signs of the bear—rocks overturned, moss dug up, dead trees scratched open in the search for insects, etc.

That night I put up the wooden winter storm panels across the screen porch and set up my bed inside. No sign of the bear during the night.

Friday, June 23: No sign of the bear today. We begin to hope he had departed to other islands far away. Frank Penfold arrived to put new screen in the patio door destroyed by the bear on Wednesday. I went back to sleeping on the porch.

Saturday, June 24: Another peaceful night. For the first time since Wednesday Patricia and I felt it was safe to leave the island together in our canoe. Shortly after noon, when we came back for lunch, Tom McConnell telephoned to say that he had just seen the bear swimming from his island to ours and that he could see the bear out on the west side of our island even as he spoke. A few minutes later Patricia looked up and saw through the patio door the bear beside the woodpile not more than ten feet from the cottage. I chased out after it and followed it to a large open rocky area in the middle of our island, but then lost sight of it when it went into the bushes.

McDonald came over again armed with the only weapon in the neighborhood, a 22 caliber rifle. We had been told that a 22 is useless against bears—all such a small bullet does when it strikes is anger the bear—still it is what we had. Pete and I circled the island twice in his boat to see if we could see the beast. No luck, and I told Pete that all we might have done is to insure that the bear did not swim away from our island! He telephoned an old friend on the mainland, Carman Emery, with whom Pete once went hunting for wolves. Mrs. Emery said that Carman was off in the bush and that, in any event, they did not want any bear meat. No help from that direction. That night I slept inside the cottage again with the storm shutters up on the porch. No sign of the bear, however.

Sunday, June 25: Comforted by the uneventful night, Patricia and I paddled off to have morning coffee with the Erdmanns on the front porch of their cottage on E 27. We left our cottage closed and with the storm panels up on the porch. In addition I drove nails through some old pieces of plywood to place, point side up, on the steps outside the patio door in an effort to discourage the bear's possible approach. I also made, at Patricia's insistence, what we hoped would be a scary drawing of a large human head and pasted it on the glass patio door (the idea being that it might serve not as a scarecrow, but a scarebear!). We had a nice paddle and enjoyed our coffee with George and Sue. Even as we sat on their porch we saw a bear on the shore of E 19 across the channel. It ambled off as we watched. We felt encouraged that the bear was over there and not on our island! Finally, before noon, we paddled home. As we landed the canoe we heard a thump and looked up to see that a storm shutter had been torn off and the screen on the porch ripped out. As we ran up from the canoe landing we realized that the bear was still inside our cottage—we could hear him moving around. At this point we were concerned to get him to exit the way he had entered and not to force his way out causing still more damage to the cottage. Patricia went around back so that the bear would see her through the patio door and I withdrew from the front. In a moment the bear came, as we had hoped, bounding out through the torn screen. I dashed inside to grab the 22 which McDonald had left with us and went after the bear. He stopped to watch me on the path in front of our cottage and I took aim— no mean feat for someone who has only held and fired a gun once in his life and that was about 46 years earlier when I had been in the ROTC (Reserve Officer Training Corps) at university. Before I could be sure that my aim was true, the bear turned and went off into the bushes again.

Back to the cottage to survey the damage and clean up mess. Once onto the porch the bear had gotten up on my bed, slid back the screen on the window between the porch and the kitchen, and leapt through that small window onto the kitchen sink, knocking over and smashing the chimney on the kerosene lamp by my bed in the process. Inside he had knocked over the table, cleaned out margarine and breakfast cereal again, eaten all our supply of raisins and all our apples and had scattered garbage over the floor. After the first break-in we had laundered and scrubbed; this time we simply swept up. This was the low point for us. We were so discouraged that we debated closing the cottage and leaving the next day to return to St. Paul.

McDonald returned determined to go after the bear with his 22. He did find it on the west side of our island and got off a shot which he thinks hit the animal, but it simply vanished yet again into the bush. We, in desperation, telephoned Frank Penfold and he explained again why it would be impossible to trap the bear. He did offer to loan me his 30 caliber carbine, but I felt that I would be unable to do anything effective with it and declined. At that point Tom McConnell came by and advised me to change my mind and accept Frank's gun. As he said, the bear was only coming for our cottage and I was the only one who stood a good chance of shooting it. I telephoned Frank back and, good scout that he is, he insisted on running all the way out, despite the fierce wind, to bring me the rifle (a half hour run in his boat).

I put the storm shutter back up over the torn screen and nailed a 2 x 4, with the largest nails I could find, to keep it securely in position. When Frank arrived he gave me a hasty lesson in how to load and fire the carbine. Since its bullets can carry for more than a mile, he advised setting up a bait near the cottage but placed so that, should I fire, only an uninhabited island and open water would be in my line of fire—in every other direction there are cottages out of sight but within that mile radius. Using what was left of the peanut butter and some bacon grease I set up my bait near our canoe landing in front of the cottage. Then I sat down to wait with the carbine across my knees. Frank had advised allowing the bear to go to the bait once at least before trying a shot in order to permit the bear to get used to my standing at the cottage door with the gun.

While we ate our supper on the front porch that evening, there was a sudden sound at the patio door 20 feet away. Patricia jumped up causing her chair to fall over with a crash. There was the bear trying to get in once again and once again he had ripped out the new screening that Frank had just put in on Friday. Another night inside the cottage for me with all doors and windows closed and locked.

Monday, June 26: Another night with fitful sleep, but no sign of the bear. A telephone call from McDonald across the bay told us that, while he and Linda were having breakfast a bear broke into a storage shed behind their cottage and destroyed their compost bin. He was going to run over to take back his 22. Tom McConnell telephoned to say that he was running into the mainland to borrow a big rifle equipped with a telescopic sight and would return about noon. I resumed watch over the bait with the carbine.

Shortly after lunch, about 1 p.m., Shirley McConnell telephoned to say that she could see the bear on the west side of our island again. A few minutes later she telephoned a second time to say that the bear was moving in our direction, headed towards our canoe landing. Her call was barely concluded when we could see the bear through the window. It paid no attention to the bait at all but was headed directly for the cottage. All our plans were given up on the spot and I went out on the rock in front of the cottage. As I moved out in front, the bear was circling towards the back and his favorite patio door. I followed him around. On the patio he stopped to sniff at the plastic sun shower bags lying on the rock to heat water for our showers. I pulled the carbine up, determined to get off a shot while we were so close to one another. Instead of the loud report I expected when I squeezed the trigger, there was only a click—for some reason there was no cartridge in the chamber! The bear heard the noise, looked up at me, and walked slowly off into the bushes behind our privy.

At this moment George arrived in his boat to tell us that a bear had just been at his compost bin next to his cottage. And then Tom McConnell pulled up in his boat with his borrowed rifle. After a brief consultation we decided that George and I would head into the center of our island in an effort to encourage the bear to head back out to the west side, while Tom would go in his boat to the channel between our two islands in the hope of getting off a shot. We were to stay east of a fallen tree whose roots, now vertical, made a conspicuous landmark on the west side of our island and Tom would only shoot to the west of those roots. After a few minutes walk I decided to head back to our cottage as I was concerned about Patricia being there by herself. George decided to circle still farther east along that shore. As I approached the cottage I heard Tom fire, but I could not see him. George thought I had fired and came running. Cautiously the two of us made our way towards the fallen tree. There we found Tom who had landed his boat still farther out on that west side of our island. He told us that his shot had hit the bear, but that he had then lost sight of it. We thought the bear must be in the bushes wounded and we were not eager to plunge in after it.

Tom then noticed that Shirley was standing outside their cottage with binoculars. He shouted to her to see if she had noticed where the bear had gone. To our surprise she called back that the bear had fallen into the water and was even now swimming towards Tom's boat. And that is where we found it, wounded and trying to climb up the rocks on the shore. Tom dispatched the creature with another shot (fig. 3:23).

I think we all felt both sad at the death of this magnificent animal and relief that our ordeal was over. Islanders converged on our island at once to share in this sense of deliverance and to see the cause of all our troubles. While the Ministry authorizes the killing of nuisance bears, the rules also stipulate that the body must be disposed of. They do not say how! What was to be done with this carcass? Tom telephoned the owner of the rifle to see if he wanted the meat, but found no interest. McDonald then

3:23. The end of the "nuisance" bear. Tom McConnell ends our ordeal, 1995

asked me if he could skin it—he had once skinned a rattlesnake killed on his island and wanted to try his hand at this. His sister, Ben Baker, volunteered to help him. I tied a rope around the bear's neck and, with great difficulty, towed the remains to a distant shoal where I dragged the carcass up on a low ledge out of the water. The bear was a young male. I would guess about 2 or 3 years of age—we are to receive a report on its exact age to be determined from an analysis of one of its teeth which we took into the Ministry in Parry Sound, as per instructions. Since I could (with difficulty) drag it up out of these water, I guess that it could not weigh more than 150-200 lbs. Pete and Ben spent the rest of that afternoon crouched on the shoal recovering the pelt.

Tuesday, June 27: A wonderfully peaceful night! At 7:45 a.m. George arrived to take Patricia with him to shop for supplies in Parry Sound. We had decided before the bear was shot that one of us would have to be in the cottage at all times and so had arranged for this trip without me. Despite the death of the bear we had decided to go ahead with this plan as we could not be absolutely certain that we had been dealing with only one bear and because the two of us had not had time during these hectic days to prepare for our customary shopping expedition. As George landed to pick up Patricia he told us that he had news— there was indeed another bear! At 5 a.m. a bear had destroyed his compost bin. I ran out to check ours and discovered that a bear had been at it over night and had taken off the lid. Our sense of euphoria evaporated at once! George, as inept with firearms as I, borrowed a rifle in town that day. Now there were three of us with powerful guns. George was to spend several nights with the loaded gun beside his bed. That night I telephoned my sister Betsy who had been planning on coming up to stay in the bunk house alone. After I told her of our adventures, she cancelled her trip!

Thursday, June 29: After a day with no sign of bears George spotted two little cubs climbing a pine tree on Fayola (B 987). This means that there is a female bear here and one hears that the females are far more testy than the males, nor do they roam so widely.

Friday, June 30: The cubs were seen swimming across the channel from Fayola to E 19. The mother bear was not observed.

Saturday, July 1: George reported that he was roused from sleep at 3 a.m. by the sound of a great splash, as if a large animal had just gone into the water off his island. It was too dark to make anything out, however. This turned out to be the last sign of bears in our islands for this summer, at least.

Sunday, July 2: 11:00 a.m., I preached at the service of the Florence Universal Church in Pointe au Baril. My texts were 1 Kings 19:1-21 and Luke 9:51-62. To no one's surprise, the bear appeared as an illustration in my sermon! Tom and Shirley McConnell were part of the congregation that morning. I think we were all thankful that this episode was behind us.

Wednesday, July 5: 7 p.m., the McDonalds threw a party for all in our community to celebrate the end of the siege. The story has spread: a couple from far afield turned up for the party, eager, it seems, to see the skin. Tom has been approached by a woman whose cottage is some 5 miles away to ask if he would come and shoot a bear which has been disturbing her garbage can! We hope that the party truly marks the end of our bear troubles! Much has been learned by us all. Never again will we leave our cottage without closing all doors and windows. If only we had prevented the bear from getting in that first time! We now know that they are diurnal, and that they are extremely curious animals, that they are guided almost exclusively by their sense of smell and are attracted by any strong odors whether from things edible or not (our mothballs and soap were disturbed), and that once they have found a source of food they never forget and will continue to return, sometimes for years. Our hope is that we might discover some way to deal with such a problem, should it ever happen again, without the anarchy of rank amateurs wandering around with highly dangerous weapons!

Despite our troubles and the destruction of the McDonalds' and Erdmanns' bins it was not until the following summer when another bear broke in that we finally understood the danger of composting! In 1996, on the morning our daughter and her family were preparing to leave, they found a bear under the table on the front porch. It had torn open the screen at one end to enter, a hole at the other end to depart. The bear devoured dry cereal that had been packed and left on the porch and opened plastic bags containing dirty diapers. These it scattered here and there. This same bear was seen by Hope later that afternoon near the outhouse after she and Bob arrived. I then discovered that our compost bin had been demolished, presumably by this same bear. To our great good fortune this bear did not return and we learned our lesson. No longer will any of us compost garbage! Today we store such waste inside the cottage until we are ready to take it to Pointe au Baril. As another consequence of our experience Patricia and I decided to have our cottage clad with steel siding. We hope such a barrier may discourage bears from trying to tear open the fragile walls!

4:24. F. C. Carter on his island, Belle Chasse, in 1914

CHAPTER FOUR

Our Pioneers, 1913-1919

For some reason the purchase of islands in our area begins very suddenly in 1913. Before that year was out the following purchases were registered in Parry Sound: on October 16 Miss Fuller B 935, on October 31 Mr. C. G. French B 937, on December 4 Mr. F. C. Carter B 995, and on December 26 Miss Florence Diehl B 945. The actual process of selecting an island and arranging for the purchase seems to have taken place over the summer, 1913. Gary French tells of two of those purchasers, his grandfather and Mr. Carter.

> My grandfather articled at the law firm of Mason Foulds in Toronto from 1910 until he graduated in 1913.
>
> Fred Carter articled with him at Mason Foulds and they worked for Gershom W. Mason. Mr. Carter worked for some Americans at an island around the Ojibway and subsequently ended up with that island which has remained with his family today through his daughter, Mrs. Mary Ortved. (139A - Wawonaissa).

4:25. Charles and Mabel French at the island, ca. 1914

Mr. Mason had owned an island up Ugo-Igo Channel and told his two articling students about the availability of islands in what we know as the French's Bay area. Fred Carter subsequently bought island B 995 and named it Belle Chasse (fig. 4:24)...The first time my grandfather went up to the island he paddled out from Pointe au Baril station. (Robert A. Bergs writes that he had heard from Gary's father that Carter and French "when the islands were first opened for public ownership...travelled together in the caboose of a freight train from Toronto to Pointe au Baril in search of the islands that they would claim...)

My grandparents used to go to the island in the summers from the Muskoka cottage because they enjoyed the peace and tranquillity of the area. My grandmother fished and my grandfather was pretty much content on just chopping some wood and cooking, as well as canoeing. They camped there before purchasing Sagastaweekee, a Cree name meaning House of Sunshine, for $163 (fig. 4:25). They saw the area as a true getaway from society and the social environment of Toronto and Muskoka. I think they saw themselves as nomadic pioneers!

Robert A. Bergs, the current owner of Mr. Carter's Belle Chasse, has provided a copy of the original patent for that island. On it is recorded the date of sale, July 10, 1913; the date of the patent is August 13, and the sale was recorded on December 4. Mr. Carter did not build on his island despite the requirement to do so within 18 months of purchase, but he did camp there with his friends over the next few years. Here is the text of the patent:

> Province of Ontario. George the Fifth, by the Grace of God, of the United Kingdom of Great Britain and Ireland, and of the British Dominions beyond the Seas, King, Defender of the Faith, Emperor of India, to all to whom these presents shall come– Greeting: Whereas Frederic Charteris Carter of the City of Toronto in the County of York, Barrister-at-Law has contracted and agreed for the absolute purchase of the Lands and Tenements hereinafter mentioned and described, at and for the price or sum of Eighty one dollars of lawful money of Canada, and of which Lands We are seized in right of Our Crown; Now Know Ye, that in consideration of the said sum of Eighty one dollars well and truly paid to Our use at or before the sealing of these Our Letters Patent, We have granted, and by these Presents do grant unto the said Frederic Charteris Carter in fee simple: All that Parcel or Tract of Land situate, lying and being in front of the Township of Shawanaga in the District of Parry Sound in the Province of Ontario, containing by admeasurement Five and six tenths acres be the same more or less, which said Parcel or Tract of Land may be otherwise known as follows, that is to say, being composed of Island B 995 situate in the Georgian Bay of Lake Huron in front of the said Township of Shawanaga as shewn on plan of survey by Ontario Land Surveyor David Beatty dated Nineteen hundred and eleven of record in the Department of Lands Forests and Mines a copy of which plan is also of record in the office of the Local Master of Titles at Parry Sound.

> Saving, excepting and reserving, nevertheless, unto Us, Our Heirs and Successors, all pine trees standing or being on said lands, together with the right to enter upon said land to remove said timber; also reserving all ores, mines or minerals which are or shall hereafter be found on or under said land, and the free

4:26. One of our "pioneers"–Carrie Zahn Bartow

use, passage and enjoyment of, in, over and upon all navigable waters which shall or may hereafter be found on or under, or be flowing through or upon any part of the said Parcel or Tract of Land hereby granted as aforesaid, and reserving also right of access to the shores of all rivers, streams and lakes for all vessels, boats and persons, and subject also to the provisions of the Act to preserve the forests from destruction by fire and of any special regulations which may be made regarding the use of fire or protection therefrom, and subject to the following conditions, namely: (1) No pine timber on the said land shall be cut except for necessary building or clearing, and then only with the written permission of the Minister of Lands, Forests and Mines of Our said Province of Ontario, and in case any such timber is cut without authority as aforesaid, such cutting shall be deemed a trespass and shall subject the offender to the penalties prescribed by the Crown Timber Regulations, and all such timber so cut shall be paid for by the grantee at such prices as may be fixed by the said Minister. (2) Where timber is cut all the debris, tops, branches and other refuse matter caused by such cutting shall be cleaned up and removed or destroyed by fire or other-

4:27. Other early cottagers ready for a swim in the 1920s,
(l. to r.), Leonard Giovannoli, Lucy Young, Gladys Dickey

wise. (3) The said grantee shall within eighteen months from the date hereof expend not less than three hundred dollars in the construction of buildings or on other improvements. (4) No building or other construction shall be erected unless the plan and description thereof have been approved by the said Minister. (5) In default of compliance with any of the above provisoes or conditions the said Minister may cause the said lands to be forfeited. Given under the Great Seal of Our Province of Ontario, Witness: His Honour Sir John Morison Gibson, Knight Commander of Our Most Distinguished Order of St. Michael and St. George, a Colonel in Our Militia of Canada, etc., etc., etc., Lieutenant-Governor of Our Province of Ontario. At Our Government House, in Our City of Toronto, in Our Province of Ontario, this thirteenth day of August in the year of Our Lord one thousand nine hundred and thirteen, in the Fourth year of Our Reign. By Command of the Lieutenant-Governor in Council. (Signed by the Provincial Secretary and the Deputy Minister of Lands, Forests and Mines.)

After these first four islands were purchased in 1913 the next to be recorded are those of Carrie Zahn, B 919, (September, 1914) and Lucy Young, B 918, (August 27, 1915). Carrie, of Buffalo, New York, was married on April 3, 1915, to Chester Bartow and that summer began a diary which she kept until 1976 (fig. 4:26). From its pages one learns that she spent her first month in our islands as the guest of Florence Diehl on the latter's island, B 945, in the summer of 1914. The owner of the adjacent island, B 944, (which has now reverted to crown land), the Reverend E. Burgess Brown, recommended that she buy B 919. This she did, paying $20 for a survey and then $10 per acre to purchase the 1.9 acre island. By June, 1915, she had had Olver Reid build a small klondike cottage for her—it was two rooms, the first 16 feet by 10 feet with a 7 by 10 kitchen attached. Here she and her new husband spent that summer from June until August 29. Their only boat was a 19 foot Carlton canoe.

By the end of the Bartows' first summer on the island they named Inverurie, Lucy Young, who had been at Olver Reid's Islander Camps that summer, had purchased the next island to the south, B 918. The following summer she occupied her own new cottage there. Sometime, in the 1920s, my aunt Gladys Dickey prepared a map of Lucy's island (see page xiii) where she had been a visitor that first summer of 1916 (fig. 4:27). She wrote the following legend on this map:

> WATAHWASO—The summer home of Miss Lucy H. Young in the waters of Georgian Bay in the region south of the Ojibway Hotel. One acre in size Domain of George the Fifth. (Several features she illustrates are labeled): a group of trees, Dense woods; in front of the cottage a figure carrying buckets, Water was obtained in this way the first summer; to the right of the cottage at the base of a pine tree, Garden was started here; on a point near the dock, Bathing here at sunrise is delightful; off the island itself, at the right margin, a fishing pole and line, Emma's island (a visiting friend of Lucy's)

The Bartows were not there that summer; in fact, after 1915, they did not return until July, 1919, by which time they were accompanied by Chester Bartow, Jr., not quite one year old. He had been born the August before and Carrie writes of his first visit in 1919,

4:28. The original French cottage on B 937

"we took him everywhere in our canoe!"

Two more islands in our group were purchased in 1919, B 962, Fireplace or Divided Island, which has never been occupied, and B 987, Fayola. Ernest Pope wrote to me in 1989 to recall the two islands his father purchased in 1919. I shall quote the preamble to his letter as it captures some of the humor I always associate with Ernie.

I will be 79 on St. Patrick's (1989) and don't like the idea except when I consider the alternative, and age has been taking its toll, with more visits to doctors (thank God at least not dentists— they're already paid for, so no more cavities), especially oph- thalmologists, optometrists, opticians etc., because in addition to incipient cataracts, I have "macular degeneration," which I never even heard of until last year: progressive and irreversible worsening of the macula, the area in the middle of the retina which sees the fine stuff so I have to use the best reading glass- es and a big magnifying glass to read a newspaper column, and this rusty typewriter because by now my handwriting is almost impossible for both the reader and the writer. Cause and cure are unknown, as is why some men get bald prematurely while others keep a good head of hair all their life; but I'd rather be bald than blind, but unfortunately have no choice, and if I live long enough no doubt will end up being both...

My father bought B 987, Fayola, and 395 A, Minnissabik, in 1919, and we lived on Minnissabik because we had only a canoe and a rowboat and it was nearer the Ojibway and Perks put up a 12 by 20 shack on it.

Meanwhile, back on Sagastaweekee Mr. and Mrs. French, perhaps tired of camping, had a one room cottage, 12 by 14, built in that same year, 1919 (fig. 4:28). This room constitutes part of the present cottage of Pete and Linda McDonald. Gary French continues the story:

> Early on, my grandparents used to rent a boat that would bring them out from Scott's Livery in Parry Sound. All the food was bought at Simpson's and shipped to Scott's so that there were provisions for ten days to two weeks. It used to take about 3 hours in the slow launch to cover the 35 miles from Parry Sound to the island. The launch always towed out two canoes, one green and one red. The canoes were left at Scott's Livery. When my great grandparents would come to visit (those were my paternal great grandparents), they would take the train to Pointe au Baril and stay at the Ojibway and then go out to the island from there...

> One of the best early stories that Dad recollects is his grandfather, Dr. Hay, having dinner at the Ojibway. One of the maids had a sudden attack of appendicitis. Dad's grandfather, Dr. Stephen Moffatt Hay, was one of the country's leading general surgeons of the day.

> He took the maid into the kitchen and with kitchen knives, he operated successfully by oil lamp and removed the aforementioned appendix.

Strictly speaking I should conclude this chapter at this point because the next island purchase was not recorded until November 25, 1920 when the ownership of B 945 was transferred from Florence Diehl to Harry Giovannoli. But the history of the Giovannoli family in the area goes back to 1908 or 1909 and those beginnings belong

4:29. The Giovannoli boys at Reid's Islander Camp in 1915

here. During his eighty-seventh year Harry's son, Leonard, went through his papers and photographs and wrote an account to be quoted here and continued in the next chapter. At his age he found the process both difficult and painful, as he mentioned in a letter accompanying his essay.

> My house is crowded with STUFF, all sorts of stuff and finding anything can be a very frustrating, time consuming effort. What I have found has sometimes surprised me, things I had no idea that I had. Things I knew I had seem impossible to locate. And then reading thru a lot of stuff to find something worth sending to you.

> Worst of all has been the emotional reaction. Now over 80 years after my father's first visit to the Bay, I am reviewing practically my whole life. Of course my life has been very good by many standards but it has also had its losses. It may surprise you to learn that I am the last Giovannoli...Since my father's first trip to Georgian Bay I have lost all my family...Not a single Giovannoli left. A review of our visits to Georgian Bay covers the loss of practically all my kin. (Elsewhere he mentions one of those losses, his brother Bob killed in 1936.)

4:30. Leonard and Bob Giovannoli and the Klondike cottage at the Camp, 1915

The Story of the Giovannolis on Georgian Bay, Ontario, 1909-1965
(as I, Leonard Giovannoli, remember it in 1989)

Some time about 1908 my father, Harry Giovannoli, an ardent small mouth black bass fisherman, heard thru friends of a similar taste about the fine fishing on Georgian Bay and about the Ojibway Hotel. After a trip or two he took my mother up there once but left the children at home. Not much more fishing was done (because Leonard's mother died in 1913 when he was 11) until 1915 when my father took my brother and me along for a two weeks' fishing trip in the Bay. At that time Olver Reid was operating a small "outpost" camps and rowboats for hire, some staple supplies, about where the Sands have their camps now (fig. 4:29). He ferried fishermen in from the Railroad station, etc. How my father heard of his place I do not know. We did take advantage of these services and rented one of his "Klondike Cottages" where we camped for nearly two weeks (fig. 4:30). These were very primitive, floor and roof (tar paper), walls boarded up half way, canvas curtains above that with solid shutters to board them up in winter. No glass, no screens probably. A wood stove and cots. We rented a row boat and hired an Indian guide and really caught fish...(fig. 4:31).

4:31. Leonard was 14 that summer and 73 years later he still had the belt pictured here! 1915

5:32. Leonard after the accident. Kenusa in the 1920s

CHAPTER FIVE

First Additions, 1920-1929

For accounts of island life during this decade we have the essay of Leonard Giovannoli, the diary of Carrie Bartow, the letter from Ernest Pope, and the map Gladys Dickey made of the island, E 5, that she and fellow teacher, Helen Whitelaw, purchased in 1922. While Leonard's and Ernie's accounts cover a period extending beyond 1929, I have decided that it is best to complete their stories in this section.

Between the two week visit in 1915 and the purchase of Miss Diehl's island in 1920, Leonard's father Harry remarried. Leonard's stepmother was named Polly and her sister, Fanny, married an older man, Anderson Gratz, who had a cottage on Ugo-Igo where Leonard was sometimes a guest. Another member of the Giovannoli family resident on B 945 over the years was Harry's unmarried sister, Olive. Their first summer in the newly acquired cottage was probably 1921 when Leonard was 19. By this time he had lost his left leg, amputated just below the hip after an accident (fig. 5:32). For the rest of his

5:33. The cottage on Kenusa after the front porch was added
but before the side porch was added, early 1920s

life Leonard relied on two crutches with whose aid he went
everywhere.

> There was already on the island (B 945) one of the so-called
> Klondike Cottages. My father or the previous owner made
> improvements and additions, boarded up the sides to the eaves
> and added windows that could be raised and hung to the rafters
> inside. We added a porch across the entire front and screened
> it in (fig. 5:33). A few years later an additional porch was added
> on the side towards the water. This furnished a "bedroom" for
> us boys. (Before the addition Leonard and his brother Bob slept
> in a tent pitched near the cottage; once the porch was built the
> tent was used to house a regular guest, Dr. James H. Taylor, a
> Presbyterian minister, mentioned later.) The other end of the
> porch, around the corner was the bedroom for my aunt, my
> father's sister. My father and his new wife slept inside.
> Somewhere along the line a small porch was added in the back
> and many years later this was enlarged.
>
> Our camp was entered almost every winter, sometimes by
> thieves and sometimes perhaps just to be used as a camp. We

5:34. The first Giovannoli motorboat and an early outboard motor,
(l. to r.), Bob, Leonard, Polly, Aunt Olive, Harry, early 1920s

seldom lost anything of much value because we left so little there. This was a nuisance. Finally we built a closet, not large but deep; the inner 2 and 1/2 feet was fixed so it could be partitioned off by a false wall. Behind that wall we stored everything we really valued. Neither thieves nor mice ever found their way in.

Bathing facilities were a hand basin, an old fashioned galvanized wash tub or most often a secluded cove in the Bay. Kitchen water never became more handy than a bucket and the dock and a strong back.

Where and when our first boat, a St. Lawrence River Skiff, appeared on the scene I do not know. It may have come with the camp. We soon had a canoe, Old Town, 16', brought from home. Our first motor boat was ordered the first year we were all there. It cost $75 delivered. It turned out to be a horribly heavy, squarish, flat bottomed wood boat, stern square for carrying an outboard motor (fig. 5:34). It was built for us over the winter by Mose and Felix Laramie of Penetanguishene, Ontario. They are worth a story all by themselves. Two old brothers, French

5:35. Mose Laramie at the door of the log cabin he and his brother built
on B 858, mid 1920s

5:36. The Laramie brothers and their boat from Penetanguishene,
(l. to r.), Mose, dog Chico, Felix, 1922

5:37. Leonard in the Richardson Special, late 1920s

Canadians; Mose, who had lost a foot, did all the talking and cooking and the thinking and Felix who seldom spoke unless spoken to but did all the work. Later they built a small log cabin on a far corner of Charlie Anderson's Island (B 858) in which they lived during the working season (fig. 5:35). Before that they bunked in a crude cabin on a small motor boat (fig. 5:36). They migrated up the Bay in the spring for the available work, returning in the fall to Penetanguishene. Mose could cook a nice loaf of bread.

But to get back to the boat, it was strong but that was all you could say good about it. Dad, neither boatman nor mechanic, had bought a primitive outboard motor, 1 and 1/2 hp. with a square gas tank around the flywheel. There was a knob on the

5:38. Leonard and the sloop he sailed from Florida in 1939

flywheel with which you rocked the piston back and forth a few times and then gave it a big jerk to start it. As often as not it would not start or it would back fire and the flywheel would turn in reverse and very often hit your thumb before you could get it out of the way. When it did run it was of course much too small for the heavy boat. Even my Dad could see that it was a horrible combination. It was that fall I think that Dad ordered our Richardson Special which served well for many years (fig. 5:37). It was slow and sometimes hard to start but it looked mighty good to us. It too was a bit under-powered but who cared. We were seldom in a hurry. It lasted us to about the end of our time in the Bay. We never had another boat. I had other boats but only once brought one to the Island, all the way from Florida. (A sloop which he sailed up in 1939, fig. 5:38) But that is another story.

Eventually the subject of a name for the island came up but ideas were few. Finally a guest, a fine preacher from Washington, D.C. (Dr. James Taylor) suggested "Kenusa," short for Kentucky, U.S.A., our state of residence at that time. No one could do any better so from then on we spoke of our island as Kenusa.

5:39. The Church Service in 1922, (l. to r.), back row: Leonard, unknown lady, Aunt Olive, Millie Anderson, Clark Anderson, Bob, Charlie Anderson, Dr. J. H. Taylor, Miss Fuller; front row: Lucy Young, Polly, Peggy Hamilton

This preacher, of Scottish origin, was a very fine man. He had been our favorite when we lived in Washington, D.C. My mother, a daughter of a Scottish Presbyterian preacher, picked his church and he and my father became very good friends. He visited Kenusa several times and the pleasure was mutual and abundant. Every Sunday nearly when he was there he held a sort of church service on some attractive island. The word was spread and generally we had 12 to 15 people to attend a simple service (fig. 5:39). Miss Fuller and Peggy Hamilton our nearest neighbors, Lucy Young, and the Andersons were faithful attendants. We all gave thanks for the obvious.

My father came up to FISH (fig. 5:40). He was no boatman so if he went fishing that meant someone had to go with him, usually me. I enjoyed the boating, even the rowing, if he felt inclined to troll. We mostly still fished with worms for bait but if the bass did not respond soon we did troll from the rowboat. We never fished from the motorboat. Trolling produced pike usually but sometimes nice bass, too. Often, if we got a pike, we threw it

5:40. Harry Giovannoli (center) "came up to FISH" The "limit" in the early 1920s, (Dr. Taylor, l., and Bob, r.)

out on the rocks for the gulls. As you know the pike had an odor and we did not consider them fit to eat. Much later tho when the bass were scarce we changed our mind about that and did eat pike but only after much scraping of the skin to rid it of the mucus which seemed to carry the odor. We ate fish most every day and never seemed to tire of that. In early times it was the only fresh meat available. We never had any refrigeration except a box under the house on the shady side. Fishing worms were kept alongside in a box of moss.

After flopping around aimlessly for several years in college I finally decided that I wanted to major in zoology and from then on I made bird lists and observations, pickled frogs and small fish, made museum skins from mice and other small mammals. Even wrote a few bits for the local sheet the Pointe au Baril Islanders' Association got out in the summer. I tried to take pictures with nothing but an ordinary Kodak; the results were certainly very primitive.

I did have the luck to catch some stickle-backs in the Beaver Pond on Big Island (E 54). They are not exactly a rare fish but I have never seen any before or since. They are named from the

5:41. First summer in residence on E 5,
(l. to r.), Gladys Dickey, Kate Whitelaw, Helen Whitelaw, 1926

several conspicuous spines in their dorsal fin. They have very interesting habits during their spawning, making a sort of bower for a nest. It would be interesting to see if they are still to be caught there. They are no more than two or three inches long.

During the early years of our summers on Georgian Bay my father was editor of a newspaper, a work he enjoyed next to fishing. In fact I have seen him fishing in a sort of absent-minded way and now and then he would say something that indicated that he had been thinking about problems in his newspaper work. He could not get his work completely out of his mind even when fishing. Being this way he was interested in getting mail in and out frequently. That suited me. I preferred a trip in our boat any time over fishing. In those years there were fewer boats. We had neighbors without a motorboat. That furnished me with an opportunity to visit and do some favors. I would post and get mail for others and even shop for groceries for them at times. One of my best customers was a well-to-do retired steel man from Makee, Pennsylvania. He was a big man with a big

5:42. Camping on B 995 before any cottage built. Bertha Howell, friend of Gladys Dickey, and her tent where the Bergs' cottage now stands, 1926

appetite, six eggs for breakfast, etc. One time he asked me to get him a steak, a thick one. I can't remember his name but I will never forget the reply he gave me when I asked how thick. He held up his hand flat with the thumb across the palm and said, "That thick." That sounded like a roast to me but that was what I got. In those days we did not worry about cholesterol. He had purchased the home of Mr. Anderson's brother on the same island as Charlie lived on.

I wonder how many people today can remember a funny thing that happened up at Carolyn Island. We were having a group picnic. People were coming in several boats including Miss Young in her handsome, big canoe. Most of us were already ashore when she expertly brought her canoe up along a very good natural rock landing. Her passengers all got out while she and perhaps others held the canoe. For her to get out of a canoe was no trivial matter and she should have had more help, but somehow she did not. She put both hands on the rock and then partially succeeded in getting up on her feet and hands. For some reason her help failed her at this moment. With considerable of her weight on her hands the canoe began to move away from the rock. She could not get her weight off her hands nor could she pull the canoe back in against the rock. Slowly but steadily the canoe moved out of reach of would-be help. No boat hook was handy. There just was nothing that anyone could do. She stretched farther and lower, her feet caught in the canoe and her hands on shore. It was just like her to be laughing all the while. It was funny. The inevitable finally did happen. She was almost stretched flat when she could no longer hold herself up and dropped in with a big splash. Helping hands could then give her a lift out of the water and somehow the canoe was recovered and all was well except she was soaked. No real harm was done.

As I mentioned earlier, my aunt, Gladys Dickey, an elementary school teacher in St. Louis and her friend Helen Whitelaw who taught history in a high school in the same city had been guests of Lucy Young. In 1922 they pooled their resources and purchased the small island E 5 north of French's Bay (fig. 5:41). Sometime between 1926 and 1928, Gladys drew a map which still hangs on the wall of our cottage on B 980. The former year is written on the map, while the later limit is fixed by the fact that she did not draw a cottage on B 995. Walter Riley had purchased that island in April, 1928 and had a cottage there by the summer. On her map she drew a tent on the spot where the future cottage was to be built and labeled it the "camp site." There, prior to 1928, her friend Bertha Howell camped (fig. 5:42). The map's style is similar to the one she made for Lucy Young already mentioned, but it differs in depicting, not one island, but the entire area covered by this history from Hemlock Channel south to Frederic Inlet. On this map, as on the other, she drew a coat of arms for each owner—hers included a money bag with wings to symbolize what she always called the "Dickey Curse," the tendency to spend whatever money came in! Written on the map, too, is the following story of their first years:

> The daring discoverer Lucy A. Young was the first to settle in this region. From her our two heroines learned how to cope with the black flies, pine beatles, and Eaton's. She initiated them into the mystic rites of Michies, the Ojibway Wharf and cleaning fish.

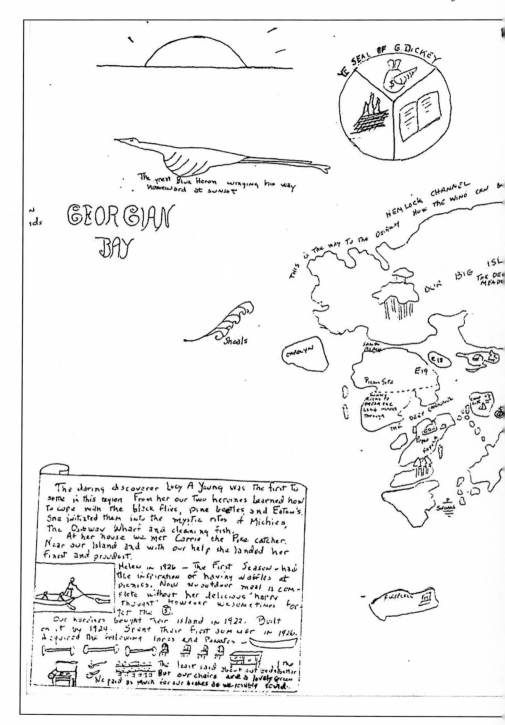

YE SEAL OF G. DICKEY

The great Blue Heron winging his way homeward at sunset

GEORGIAN BAY

N ids

HEMLOCK CHANNEL

HOW THE WIND CAN B

THIS IS THE WAY TO THE OSTRAY

OUR BIG ISL

THE DE
MEADO

Shoals

CAROLYN

SANDY BEACH

E 18

E 19

Picnic Site

THE DEEP CHANNEL

Shoals

The daring discoverer Lucy A Young was The first to some in this region. From her our two heroines learned how To cope with the black flies, pine beetles and Eaton's. She initiated them into the mystic rites of Michies, The Outway Wharf and cleaning fish.
At her house we met Carrie the Pike catcher. Near our Island dad with our help she landed her finest and proudest.

Helen in 1926 — The First Season had the inspiration of having waffles at picnics. Now no outdoor meal is complete without her delicious "happy Thought" however we sometimes forget the ⓢ.
Our heroines bought their island in 1922. Built on it by 1924. Spent their first summer in 1926. Acquired the following Inces and Penates —

The least said about our cedar better but our chairs are a lovely green. We paid as much for our boxes as we possibly could.

Fullness

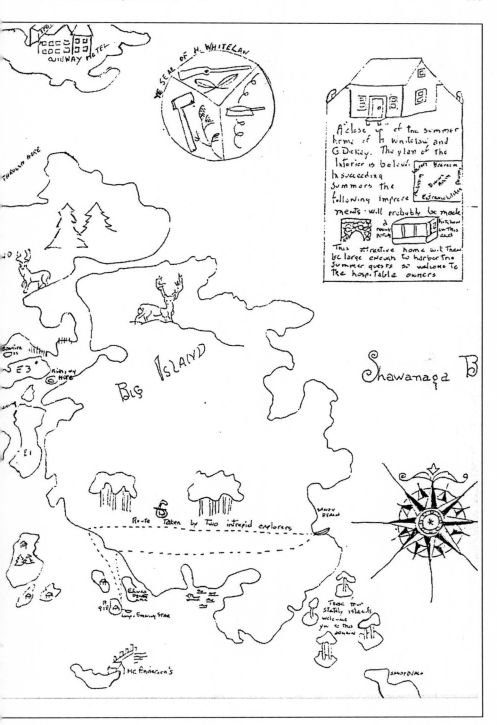

At her house we met Carrie the Pike catcher (Carrie Bartow from B 919). Near our island and with our help she landed her finest and proudest.

Helen in 1926—the First Season—had the inspiration of having waffles at picnics. Now no outdoor meal is complete without her delicious "happy thought." However we sometimes forget the salt.

Our heroines bought their island in 1922. Built on it by 1924. Spent their first summer in 1926. Acquired the following lares and penates—(there follows sketches of the canoe, cots, chairs, stove, etc.)

The least said about our beds the better. But our chairs are a lovely green. We paid as much for our dishes as we possibly could.

(In another box on the map is a sketch of the cottage described) A "close up" of the summer home of H. Whitelaw and G. Dickey. The plan of the interior is below. (The drawing depicts a one room cottage in which the function of each part of the room is labeled. There are two) bedrooms, a library, pantry, kitchen, dining room. In succeeding summers the following improvements will probably be made—(a fireplace), a roomy porch (with a) kitchen on this end. This attractive home will then be large enough to harbor the summer guests so welcome to the hospitable owners.

Gladys wrote captions for several places on the map including dotted lines across E 54 (Big Island) identified as "Route taken by two intrepid explorers." As the lines begin and end on B 918 they represent a hike taken by the two women during the time they were guests of Lucy. In the same area one reads an enigmatic comment beside the outline of island B 821 down on Shawanaga, "An unappreciated meal for two gentlemen who did not appear." I would like to know the story behind that comment! Nearer their new island she wrote on Hemlock Channel, "This is the way to the Ojibway. How the wind can blow through here." My favorite, however, is to be found next to a dotted line which marks a route across the island E 19 to those "sunny rocks" mentioned earlier.

In 1923, the summer after Gladys and Helen purchased E 5,

Lucy had Felix Laramie add a fireplace to her cottage (the chimney can be seen in the map of her island) and Paul Pope finally had a cottage constructed on his second island, B 987, Fayola. The Popes did not actually use the cottage, however, until 1924, as Ernie relates. (In this portion of his letter Ernie reveals his fondness for picturing himself as somewhat wild—a characterization which caused much talk when I was young.)

> (Dr. Pope) had Thorkildsen build the newer and bigger cottage, with fireplace, on Fayola. My father kept on teaching at Cornell to finance a 2-year European trip for my mother and Italian, German and French schools for Elfrieda and me. We returned in late summer of 1923 for my father and me to "camp" for a few weeks at Minnissabik and to buy for $300 a used Richardson Special and with it to inspect the new cottage on Fayola, to which we moved in the summer of 1924 because it was more comfortable, prettier and less traffic than in the Ugo-Igo–Kishkadena area. We had the motorboat until, while I was in Germany, (as a foreign correspondent and author of the book, Munich Playground) my father bought in 1938 the new, 4-cylinder Seabird "Fayola." We, especially I, used Minnissabik as a halfway station, as well as a place for me to entertain my favorite waitress while I was working at the Ojibway. After the shack fell into disrepair, I myself put on new sides and south roof. In 1950 I had Penfold build a new cottage connected to "Paddi's cottage" for me, wife Helen and daughter Diana. That year my father died...Happy Memories...As ever for us South (of) Carolynians, Ernie.

The Bartows managed only four visits during this decade, in 1921, 1924, 1927, and 1928. In 1927 they had an extended stay stretching from July through to October 13. Carrie comments in her diary that they picked cranberries on Blackberry Island, B 965, and speaks of a guide, Joe Francis, who took them to the Station in his big boat and shot wild ducks to give to them. In both 1927 and again in 1928 they paddled to the Ojibway via the true "Mud Channel" between E 54 and 500 A.

> 1927: The days were wonderful—even when cool. We were out

exploring the islands, cooking meals outdoors. We went through Mud Channel to the Ojibway. Lots of fun. One day we paddled to the village, going out in front of Carolyn.

1928: We went through Mud Channel to the Ojibway guided by Len Giovannoli. Lots of fun pushing through the reeds.

While the full details and consequences of a last arrival during this decade, will be found in the next chapter, I close, not with the stock market crash, nor with my birth, but with the first visit of Ethel Williams to the Bay during the summer of 1929. Her niece, Brownie Baker, recalls:

It is my understanding that Aunt Ethel spent two weeks with Dix (9 years old) at the Pope's island, Minnissabik, in 1929. She, of course, fell in love with the area, so asked Professor Pope if he would pick her an island in Mud Channel. She then had a cottage built on the highest point of the island (E18, Chinook)—all this without ever having seen the island!

6:43. Bill Donovan on his first visit to Georgian Bay
(with his mother, Dorothy Dickey Donovan) on E 5. 1931

CHAPTER SIX

Marriage and Children, 1930 - 1945

There was a flurry of activity at the beginning of this period. Gladys and Helen had, by this time, added the promised fireplace and porch. The additional space enabled Gladys to invite her younger sister Gwen Erdmann and her family, husband Morris and sons Jim and George, for a visit the summer of 1930. In 1931 she invited her youngest sister Dorothy Donovan and her family, husband Elmer and sons Dick, Bob, and Bill. I, at eighteen months, was still in diapers and have no memories of that visit. There are photographs of me touching the top of a small pine in front of the cottage and having a bath in a washtub behind (fig. 6:43). For memories I defer to my older cousins and brothers.

In the opening years of the decade Ethel Williams had a cottage built on E 18 and Helen Lewandowski purchased B 985. The period begins with a most happy occasion, the wedding of Helen to Clint Grove, and ends with the tragedy and losses of World War II.

6:44. Mr. Charles (Charlie)
Anderson holding a gull, 1920s

Recalling the happy beginning, Helen Grove tells of her purchase
and her wedding.

> My earliest memories of Georgian Bay are naturally associated with
> Ethel Williams (later Plimpton) who was our sorority advisor and my
> Spanish teacher at Western Reserve University. Because she and I
> had hit it off so well in Europe during the summer of 1928, she
> asked me to spend a month of the summer of 1929 at Cornell,
> where she had to take some courses in German towards her doc-
> torate. Her illustrious father had been sent to Hawaii by the
> government but stipulated to the young professor renting the
> Williams' home that Ethel was to have her bedroom. After being
> awakened at 5:00 every morning by the Finch children, Ethel men-
> tioned to Dr. Pope that she was in no condition to resume her

teaching duties that fall. He offered her the use of Minnissabik and she, in turn, offered me the chance to go with her. I thought that it didn't sound like my cup of tea and refused. She took her nephew Dix (McDonald), then aged nine, and they had a great time. She returned looking and feeling wonderful and announced that she "could lick the earth." She proceeded to purchase Chinook and asked Dix's father to draw up plans for her cottage. In 1930, her cottage was finished and this time I went, with young Dix, by train from Cleveland. She invited Clint Grove to spend his vacation there and he immediately became enamored of the whole thing. We got engaged then and there and since he was saving for our marriage and new home, I accepted again a summer job at Western Reserve University teaching language teachers how to teach language and earned enough to pay for the island ($140, the price based upon $20/acre for each of 5 acres, $15 for the extra .5 acre and $25 for the survey) and the cottage. Mr. Thorkildsen charged by the room—$550 for the living room, $175 for the kitchen.

Everyone, Helen Whitelaw, Gladys Dickey, Lucy Young and Mr. Riley, told me that I couldn't have island B 985 because a certain Mr. Anderson owned it and I would have to buy it from him (fig. 6:44). My father suggested that I write the Canadian government and shortly after came the reply: Mr. Anderson had paid a deposit and several years' taxes (about $2/year!!!) but did not own it. Clint and I were delighted to buy it and wrote Thorkildsen immediately to begin building our cottage, just the two rooms then. Since our vacations were limited to two weeks in those days, we would often rent the island to friends of ours for part of the summer and would then use that money for a porch, bunkhouse, posh outhouse or other improvement.

(Editor's Note: There can be no doubt that Anderson, like many others, was interested in acquiring property as an investment intending future resale. The list of islands for sale by the Department of Lands and Forests in 1926 does not include what was to become the Grove Island, B 985 and the explanation seems to be that by that time Mr. Anderson had paid a deposit on it as explained above. The official letter to Miss Helen A. Lewandowski on March 4, 1931, contains the following information: "We wish to advise that insofar as Mr. C. H. Anderson is concerned, that the Department did not com-

6:45. The Wedding Party, 1931, (l. to r.), Leonard Giovannoli, Clint Grove, Helen
Lewandowski, Gertrude Kotz, Ethel Williams, the priest (Anglican) from Parry Sound

plete the sale of the above mentioned Island (B 985) to him and
although he might have paid Taxes to this Branch, the paying of
same, does not give him any right or title to the land on which he
pays the Taxes. We have recently advised Mr. Anderson to this effect
and have also refunded to him all monies that he paid us as Taxes on
this Island, and we can readily assure you that you will not have any
further trouble in this matter as far as we are concerned." Helen's
account continues:)

> The summer of 1931 I again taught at the summer session of
> Western Reserve University and came up about the second week in
> August with my friends Blanche and Gertrude Kotz. We had been
> delayed at the border by Customs and had arrived much later than
> we had anticipated. We had ordered a large supply of food, but
> ended up going out to the island quite late with only meager provi-
> sions. We were immediately hit by a big storm which lasted sever-
> al days and took out our rowboat, the only boat we had. We were
> down to a few tea bags and the juice from a can of green beans

mixed with a little flour for sustenance. Bob Donovan (almost ten years old that summer) and his mother were fishing in Lewandowski channel and we called to them. They, being good Samaritans, returned with food and shortly thereafter, all the food we had ordered arrived. Early in September, Clint came up, stopped in Parry Sound to pick up the Anglican minister and hired a boat to come out to the island. We were married there the 5th of September (fig. 6:45). There was a Presbyterian minister on an island near the Ojibway, but he was not Canadian and the government would not recognize as valid any ceremony performed by him. We would have been considered as living in sin and in those days people cared about things like that. Shortly after our wedding, the other Islanders went back stateside and we had our honeymoon with a week of perfect late summer weather.

The following summer, I came up again with three sorority sisters until Clint could have his vacation. I had told them with pride how neatly I had left everything the summer before. We arrived to find the place infested with mice and an absolute mess. It was only Ethel's counsel that kept me from selling the place on the spot.

Images that come to mind are Kennedy's supply boat which was a wonderful institution at the time, picnics at Carolyn and bonfires at Sunset Point on Eagle (the westernmost tip of B 980). Leonard Giovannoli was part and parcel of most everything and impressed all our visitors mightily...

It is interesting to see on the weather chart for 1931 kept by Leonard that he records rain on September 4, the day before the wedding, but clear with falling temperatures on the day itself (maximum 66 and minimum 55 degrees). That is his last entry for that summer; he must have departed the day after. Brownie Baker, Ethel's niece, also recalls the wedding:

My first year with Aunt Ethel at Chinook Island must have been in 1930 when I was 6 and Dix was 10 (fig. 6:46). Pete, five years younger, didn't come for another 3 or 4 years. Grandfather Williams was usually there with us. Grandfather, Dix and I went fishing often in the old heavy green rowboat. I remember that we could hardly pull away from the dock before we had a bite, and very often a good sized one...

6:46. Dix McDonald, 11, on E
18, 1931

The most exciting occasion of my young life in Mud Channel was
the wedding of Helen and Clint Grove in their own new cottage in
1931. Ethel insisted that we wear shoes (unheard of!) and the
people and the food all looked very fancy! Leonard Giovannoli certainly was my idea of what a best man should look like—I was quite
in awe of him.

An equally exciting occasion occurred the following summer (1932)
when Aunt Ethel bought me my adored little red canoe, "ME"
(fig. 6:47). This gave me great independence, although for a few
years I didn't wander very far from Chinook.

This little red canoe we all associate with Mary Ellen (her
first two initials formed its name). In fact, many years later my

6:47. Mary Ellen (McDonald) Baker with her brother Pete in her red canoe, "ME," 1935

sister, Didge, long envious of that small craft, purchased a similar one. The original now hangs on the wall of the Baker cottage.

That summer before the wedding marked the first visit not only of Brownie Baker. George Erdmann recalls his first experiences:

> I remember just bits and pieces of our first trip to the Island; after all I was only nine that summer. It was 1930 and we had an old Model A Ford at the time. It seemed old but since the Model A was first made in 1928 it couldn't have been more than a couple of years old. Of the drive up I remember nothing—where we stopped for nights, or just how long the trip took. I do remember that we had to park the car in Parry Sound when we arrived there and take the train for the last 25 miles on to the Pointe. I have no memories of the boat trip out to the Island (it has always been "the Island" to me, whether it was E 5 where we spent our first visit, Eagle, B 980, where we vacationed from 1934 to 1937 with parts of the Donovan clan or E 3 where we spent so many wonderful years, and finally to E 27 where we bought and built in 1957. I have only two firm recollections of that first visit in 1930. The most notable was running

6:48. The Read cottage under construction in 1933

down the slope from the cottage on E 5 to, what seemed to me, an enormous dock and off into the water. The water level was high that year and just a few inches below the level of the dock. I understand that the next year someone pulled the plug and the water level dropped to the point that swimming from the dock was not possible. The second memory was so trivial but still so vivid. My brother Jim (12) and I had cots on the porch to the west side of the cottage and one evening we had our flashlights to hand and used them to watch a deermouse on the floor between our cots. I suppose the lights immobilized the mouse and we had a good look at it for some time—my first memory of wild life at the Island.

After this activity in the opening years of the decade there seems to have been a lull. The Bartow cottage was not opened at all, for example, in 1931, 1932, and 1934, and they only managed two weeks in 1933. During that same summer the Reads built on E 27 (fig. 6:48). From 1935 until 1976 Carrie did not miss a summer. Leonard's weather records are preserved for 1930, 1931, and 1932, to pick up again only in 1936 when they extend from July 10 through September 20. That same summer the Bartows remained until

September 26. In 1934, however, my parents arrived at their new cottage on B 980 whose purchase was recorded the preceding fall. At four and one half I was too young to retain any but the most fleeting of memories. Fortunately my Aunt Gladys wrote and illustrated a little book in 1935, bound with the aid of my brother Bob This book preserves a brief record of the inaugural season the summer before:

BILL AT THE ISLAND
Being His Experiences There When Four Years Old
The Bobglad Press
Kirkwood, Missouri
1935

Late one afternoon a big red motor boat brought Bill to Eagle Island for the first time. The four boys hustled Bill over the sights at the Island.

A wee little house behind a big Pine was the bedroom for Bill and Baby Sister. (The house was the bunk house; the venerable pine toppled in 1999; Baby Sister was Didge, nine months old.) There were bunks and red bookcases...Bill painted a table which was really a box. All the rocks you see were nice to sit on or to use for tables. We loved to sit under the old pine tree. Baby Sister's swing was there.

Going to the Big House to get breakfast every sunny morning. They skip over blueberries which grow in the cracks of the rocks. Billy will come in and help wake the big boys who are still asleep. He hopes they will hurry and run down to the dock to take a morning dip. He loves to watch them but he never goes in there for the water is very deep.

After this beginning the story continues with pages written in later years both by me and by Didge. That first summer my mother and her two sisters together with Didge (in a basket) and me (in a crib built by Mr. Thorkildsen) slept in the bunk house, while my father, uncle Morris, and the four boys were in the main cottage (brothers Dick 17 that summer, Bob almost 13 and cousins Jim 16 and George already 13). While it is difficult in retrospect for us to fix specific events to individual years between 1934 and 1939, the pleasures of that time are not forgotten. George Erdmann recalls:

6:49. On the trip to the island, 1934, (l. to r.), Dick Donovan, George Erdmann, Jim Erdmann, Gladys Dickey, Bob Donovan

My most complete memories of childhood at the Island occur from 1934 until 1939 when we shared cottages with the Donovans, first on Eagle and then on E 3 after it had been built on. This occurred when Aunt Gladys and Helen Whitelaw decided to divide their share of E 5. Gladys, with Dick and Bob, would drive from St. Louis to Hammond and pick up Mother, Jim and me for the trip north. Gladys had an old Essex (I believe) that she had had rigged with a picnic box holding a table, stools and other picnic gear (fig. 6:49). (This box, painted black and mounted over the rear bumper—cars of that vintage did not have trunks at the back—is still to be seen being used for storage in the cottage on E 3.) Dad built a trailer to be towed behind with all of our kit, since with 6 of us in the car there was not much other room. Jim and I built our "sea chests" out of scrap wood and these were put into the trailer with all of the other bags. These chests were ultimately put at the foot of our bunks in the cottage where we could live out of them. I can remember stopping at both old school yards and at graveyards to eat our lunch. We frequently sat on the tombstones with our peanut butter sandwiches. I have a vivid recollection of once trying to get water out of an old fashioned pump in a schoolyard and all we could pump was a mass of earthworms in very little water.

6:50. Before its transformation. The old rowboat with George and Jim Erdmann, 1934

We didn't always stop for lunches on the roadside but sometimes just picked what looked like reasonable restaurants. Each of the boys was given a dollar to eat on for the day and it was a struggle to make it through dinner with much more than a token meal. Jim invariably ran through his allowance by lunch and had to eat water and maybe a slice of bread for dinner.

It took us three days to make the trip from Hammond; the last day was mostly spent in the final few miles to Pointe au Baril. By this time the road had been completed from Parry Sound but it was partly gravel and partly just driving over sections of smoother rock. The gravel was mostly washboard and what it did to the car as well as those of us in the car was hard to describe. It was almost impossible to drive faster than 25 miles an hour. It was a long trip.

One of the early years, I'm not sure which, we stopped in Parry Sound and Aunt Gladys purchased a used double ender rowboat and a used canoe. She made arrangements to launch out to Mud Channel with old Jonas the Indian as the driver and we towed the boats all the way. It was quite a trip. I don't remember much about the trip itself but I can still see the leathery and creased face of Jonas, brown as tobacco juice (fig.2:3).

6:51. After the transformation. Under sail with Jim Erdmann, mid 1930s

Mother and Aunt Gladys tried hard but it was very hard to hold the four boys down. Weather permitting we would pack a lunch and the four of us would take off in the row boat (fig. 6:50). Soon after getting the boat we fitted it with a rudder. There were two sets of oars and with two of us rowing and one steering with one resting we could really make that boat travel. In our early years we explored the area from the Village in the north to Frederic Inlet to the south. We also made several trips to the McCoys as well as the Limestones.

Jim was the sailor in those days and it wasn't long before he had rigged a large curtain rod as a mast and boom and hung a sail on the boat (fig. 6:51). It wouldn't tack too well as there was no keel to resist sideslipping so we took the boat to Mr. Richardson in the Village and he bolted a piece of sheet metal to the keel making it sail much better. It did make it difficult to get the boat into shallow water, but we managed to live with the problem. In a couple of years the sailing rig finally went. Jim was sailing in French's Bay in a good stiff wind. I can remember that I was on the dock at Eagle watching when the boat, with a good heel on it, caught an extra heavy gust and the mast went. It had snapped in two. That ended the sail-

6:52. Sailing's Challenge!
Bob Donovan on French's
Bay, mid 1930's

ing for a while. A couple of years later I brought up a used mast and sail from an old iceboat that Jim had scrounged. It was much too heavy a mast for the boat and the sail was much too large for so narrow a boat, but it would move fast and tacked easily so that I could go wherever I wanted in the channels. That was my real start of interest in sailing that has been with me ever since.

I'm not sure what happened to that boat. After I had graduated from high school and entered into classes at Indiana University Extension Division in the Hammond-East Chicago area and, from there, went on to Northwestern University Dental School it was a long time of not going up to the Island. From 1939 until 1953 I only made it up once for a very short time in 1944 as a belated honeymoon with Sue. Sometime during that period the old boat finally gave up.

The story I heard about the four boys that first summer is that they rowed out to the McCoys without the knowledge of Gwen and Gladys. When they finally rowed back into French's Bay and saw the two anxious women pacing the rock, the boys started to sing, "Who's afraid of the big, bad wolf?" I also have many memories of that old rowboat turned sail boat. I was always terrified when taken out in it lest it capsize as it did so often (fig. 6:52). In one memorable spill, my brother Dick lost his glasses.

In 1945, when I was in 10th grade, I wrote a paper for my English class about these early years. This essay is based upon what was told to me later rather than upon my memories and I think it mixes events from more than one summer. I suspect the paper also demonstrates a fondness for making a good story better. Despite these shortcomings I'll enter it here as written, mistakes and all. Of the core I still do have some recollection. It was, I think, the summer of 1935 when my mother and baby sister left by train and my father, brothers and I followed by automobile, making the run from the island to the Station in our old, very unreliable motorboat. The title of the essay is "Water."

> Today was a day of water; every time I turned around there was something to remind me of water.
>
> The day I am speaking of dawned with a bustle of activity in the small cottage on the rock. The sun had come up from behind French's Island across the bay and the cheery sunlight fell on us as we ate a hurried breakfast on the porch. The house was a one story affair with a living and sleeping room combined, a kitchen, and a porch. The roof was covered with green tarpaper and the rough boards of the house were stained brown. The day was warm so no wind thrust its chilling fingers through the cracks and father could eat in peace without having to struggle with the curtain.
>
> Mother had gotten us up early because she and Baby Sister were leaving early on the boat from the Station while we were to come after in our old motor canoe. This was one of the saddest days in my life. We were going home from a perfect summer at the Island! But there was no time to think about it now because in the distance the roar of the approaching boat could be heard and all mother's

luggage had to be carried down to the dock along with Baby Sister in her basket.

Then the first misfortune occurred! My brother was carrying a canvas bag down to the dock. It was so big and so heavy he didn't see what he was doing and so he walked right off the end of the dock! Splash! Into the water he went bag and all and Dick in his best clothes too! But even this didn't stop us for long. We dug up some old clothes for him and fished out the bag.

As soon as mother left, the boys started to close the cottage. They swung the beds on wires from the rafters and put pie plates on them for rat guards. Meanwhile Dad and I started for the back dock to get the boat ready.

The boat was an old Sponson canoe which had seen better days. A two cylinder motor had been put in and some fancy seats, but this did not stop it from doing everything in its power to see that we didn't go any place in it.

As I sat there on the dock looking down at Dad who was working with the motor, I recalled the night less than a year ago when coming home from a supper picnic on the shoals we had run into a submerged rock that took the propeller clear off the boat, and we had to paddle the sinking boat home! The water had crept ever higher around our legs, but even then we still had fun and the people on the bay wondered what was going on what with all the singing and shouting. We finally made it home and the surprising thing was that on the next day the boys went out and found the propeller still lying on the rock!

As I was reliving that night I lay back on the dock. Suddenly I heard another splash this time from a bottle of castor oil which I had knocked over and without which our boat would not run! I got out of that locality as quickly as possible.

We finally were ready to go (9:30 a.m.). The boat had all our baggage in it and we all jumped in and cast off. Then we tried to start the engine, but without the castor oil this was almost impossible! Then we discovered water in the gasoline! By this time I was tired of the whole thing and said so. My father said afterwards that he would have thrown me overboard then and there if the engine hadn't started! We finally arrived at the Station at 4:30 p.m.! (The distance was 12 miles.)

6:53. George Erdmann with the dog, "Duke," 1937

The story my mother told was that the motor kept starting and then stalling as the boat drifted around French's Bay and every time it stalled I started to cry. Mother claimed that the fact that my father never gave me anything to eat was responsible for my tears. I do remember that we got no farther than Aurora, Ontario in what was left of that day and my father and I shared a bed for the night in the tourist home there.

My story of our old boat introduces George Erdmann's account of the summer during which we enjoyed the company of Duke. It was, I think, in 1937.

While sorting through some old pictures of life at the Island I ran across a picture of me with the dog "Duke," and it reminded me of the episode when Dick and I first found him (fig. 6:53). Dick and I

6:54. Cleaning the frosting pan. Didge Donovan and Bill outside the new cottage on E 3 with Duke hoping for a taste, too, 1937

had been on a trip in the old sponson canoe motor boat. I'll leave a detailed description of the boat to one of the Donovans, but some of its idiosyncrasies are necessary to detail to understand the events leading to the finding of Duke. We had gone to the Village for some reason that I can't remember and from there were going to the Station. The old two cylinder, two stroke engine was next to impossible to get started, even with pouring castor oil into the cylinders to increase compression. To start the engine, the fly wheel was grabbed and flipped as hard as possible. Since there was no gear box, the propeller also turned at the same time, giving the boat a small push forward. We were in the main channel leading from the Village to the Station and having no luck with starting the engine but were gradually travelling east with innumerable throws of the fly wheel, taking turns as each became exhausted. We noticed a dog on the shore of the mainland that seemed to be just following our slow movement, just keeping pace with us. We didn't give the dog much thought being too tired for any heavy mental work, but to our surprise we finally noticed that he had swum out to the boat and was right alongside. It was a good distance to the shore and we didn't have the heart to turn him away so hauled him aboard. Sometime after this we finally got the motor started and ran to the Station, did whatever business we had there and, while there, asked all around about possible ownership of the dog. No one seemed to know anything about him and had not heard of any lost dog, so finally we just took him with us back to Eagle where we were staying that year. The dog was mostly, if not all, airedale and one of the best trained and behaved dogs that I have ever known. He got along with everyone and we all grew to love him very much (fig. 6:54). One time he was in the back of the Island doing whatever dogs like to do on their own when we heard him start barking wildly. We were all on the porch of the cottage or just outside near the water when we heard him stop barking and then a streak of brown shot past us, headed for the dock and just kept going into the water where he spent several minutes just swimming around. As he ran past us it was quite obvious what the trouble was; the odor of skunk was strong and penetrating and Duke had taken a full shot. His own treatment was somewhat effective but he did maintain an aroma for some time after. I don't have any idea who named him Duke but it took him no time at all to recognize his name.

We continued to ask about ownership of the dog every time we went to the Station with no luck. Finally it was getting to the time when we were going to have to leave and it was decided that Mother and Dad would take him home with them in the car. They hadn't been gone for more than two days when an ill-tempered, foul mouthed and otherwise uncouth individual motored up to the dock in his boat, claiming ownership of Duke (naturally calling him something else). He had heard of the dog finally at the Station and wanted him back immediately. There was nothing we could do but write Mother and Dad to get him back. They had to arrange to crate him, get him what shots were necessary, and pay to have him shipped back. When his uncouth owner came to pick him up I like to think that Duke cringed at the thought of returning to his original owner.

By 1935 Pete McDonald had joined his sister Brownie and brother Dix as summer guests of their aunt on Chinook. As Pete explains:

I was born in 1930. My aunt Ethel Williams lived at our home in Shaker Heights, Ohio, when I was young. Every summer Ethel took my brother Dix, born in 1920, and my sister, Mary Ellen, "Ben" or "Brownie," born in 1924, to her island "Chinook." At five, I was first allowed to come along (fig. 6:55). We stayed all summer. I think our

6:55. The McDonald Family in 1935,
(l. to r.), Mary Ellen, Pete, Dix, their maternal grandfather Williams

parents really enjoyed their quiet summers back home.

Pete and Brownie share vivid memories of riding with Ethel in her motorboat those summers in the mid 1930s. Brownie describes the experience:

Some of my earliest (and least fond) memories concerned the weekly trip for groceries in Ethel's cedar strip outboard with the (trusty) old Evinrude motor (fig. 6:56). In those days motors did not have "reverse" or "neutral"—it was just "forward"—and one had better be pointed in the right direction! We started out from the lean-to boathouse, which Grandfather Williams had constructed on the back of Chinook Island, and we usually made it halfway out Mud Channel before the "damn motor" ever started. With each mighty (but unsuccessful) pull of the starter rope the boat lurched ahead a few feet and invariably either Dix or Pete or I would be whacked in the head by the knot at the end of the rope. With an unladylike "Damn!" Ethel would coil the rope again and we would inch our way out Mud Channel with a "Damn!" and a whack and a lurch. Often a shear pin was broken on an unmarked shoal on the way to the

6:56. Ethel Williams at the helm of her motorboat returning from the Ojibway
with Pete McDonald as passenger, 1940s

Ojibway (more cussing). But the trip seemed worth it when we got
the promised ice cream cone and were allowed to explore the
glamorous Ojibway Hotel and to marvel at the flushing johns and
electric lights. As I look back I'm really amazed that our aunt ran an
outboard at all, knowing as little as she did about boats and
motors. Most amazing was that Aunt Ethel had the courage to bring
my brothers and me to this remote area, when it really was remote!

In those years from 1936 through 1939 the young people
from the Donovan, Erdmann, and McDonald clans enjoyed almost
daily gatherings for swimming and games. Pete and I were too little
for full participation, but our presence was accepted and we much
enjoyed being allowed even minor roles in all this hilarity! The
favored locations for this activity were Chinook and Battleship (B
1000) and the water between, again as Brownie describes:

I remember wonderful parties at Helen Whitelaw's cottage with
hilarious tricks—"the magic spoon" and holding the glass of water
against the ceiling with a broom handle, and wild games of water

polo from the front dock. But Aunt Gladys was the party lady that we all loved. Many unforgettable evenings were spent in the living room at E 3 playing card games made special by Aunt Gladys' wit and sense of good fun. I still have a "Badge of Merit" cleverly made by Gladys when I first did a distance swim without a life jacket. What fun we kids had riding the old shutter surf board, until it did a nose dive and was forever buried in the mud in front of E 3. Then there was the summer that we had a running game of Monopoly at "Wabassin" (known then as "Battleship"). Bob Donovan was always the banker. The Monopoly game was usually preceded by a rowdy swim at the "swimming hole" between Chinook and Battleship, where our favorite game was to see who could capture the raft and keep all others off. This caused many painful splinters, but we all thought it was great fun. The "boys"—Dick, Jim, Dix, George, and Bob (Bill and Pete were too small to be very helpful)—built a magnificent stone and cement diving platform on Chinook at the swimming hole. It remains today, having weathered almost sixty years of fluctuating water levels without losing many stones.

Those card games were to continue for many years and a favorite was "Liverpool Rummy" consisting of six different rummy games played in sequence. One set of six could occupy us for an entire evening or a rainy afternoon. I, too, remember those swimming parties. Before I could swim in deep water I paddled about with a cork life belt strapped around my waist. One afternoon, when the young people were being "rowdy" on the raft, I got out of the water, took off my belt, and went in search of some "pine tree plumbing." On my return I dashed to the edge of the rock and jumped. In mid air I remembered that I had removed my cork belt! My brothers like to tell of pulling my thrashing body from the water, my eyes as big as saucers. To me it was a frightening experience.

Pete and I did learn to swim during the summer of 1937 in a spot called the "Roman Bath." There is a sandy bottom in the channel between E 3 and 500 A and a shoal a few yards from the shore of E 3. In low water one could wade across. I learned first to take a few strokes to get from shore to shoal, while Pete, already more adventurous, was exploring underwater (fig. 6:57). Pete also was a more active participant than I in those gatherings at Chinook, as he recalls:

6:57. Learning to swim. Bill Donovan with Gladys Dickey in the "Roman Bath," 1937

Among things that stay in my memory are: being flipped high in the air and into the water from the raft by Dix and George Erdmann and trying to help Dix build the stone diving board platform on Chinook. I rowed my big green rowboat over to Wabassin to get rocks. I filled it so full it sank...then I had to empty it and start over. I remember being allowed to play Monopoly with all the older kids, Bob Donovan, George Erdmann, Brownie and the others.

I understood that Ethel purchased B 1000 to preserve her privacy on Chinook. For us it served as the venue for those Monopoly (or as Pete used to call them "monotony") games. She had a guest cottage there as well as the bunk house on Chinook itself. Once some years later I spent a memorable night in that bunk house with Pete. What a shock the next morning to discover that I, although a guest, was expected to take the obligatory cold bath in the lake, summoned by Ethel's imperious whistle! On this occasion the famous incident of the belly button occurred. We were about to sit down to a meal on the porch when his Aunt Ethel noticed Pete was not wearing a shirt. She sent him off to get one with the injunction, "No belly buttons at the table!" (fig. 6:58) Pete recalls another episode in 1937:

6:58. The Belly Button that was not allowed at the table! Pete in front of the cottage on Chinook with his brother and aunt behind, late 1930s

When I was about seven years old, Ethel hired an Ojibway Indian to fix our docks. He brought his spouse and his seven year old son. They pitched their tent on her other island, Battleship, which housed the guest cottage. I remember chasing the Indian boy with a big ax–really playing authentic cowboys and Indians. His father quickly settled that battle by picking me up by my pants, before one of us got carried away (literally).

Brownie, too, mentions the sleeping cottages in the Williams' domain:

The original cottage on Battleship (Wabassin) was built in 1937 and I was allowed to paddle across to it to spend the night by myself. This soon became the pattern and the little cabin became my sleeping house. (The boys preferred the bunk house on Chinook.)

That next year (1938) witnessed the famous swimming race that took place off the front dock of Chinook. Despite Pete's comment, I have never claimed to have been the victor in that contest— indeed, given his prowess, I am almost certain that he was the

6:59. Who's winning? The swimming race between Pete (l) and Bill (r)
with aunts Ethel and Gladys behind, 1938

winner. Here is Pete's version:

> Aunt Gladys and Aunt Ethel arranged a swimming race between Bill
> Donovan and me. Bill still claims he won, but clearly I was ahead,
> as the picture proves (fig. 6:59).

What will always live in my memory about those summers
with Pete in the late 1930s are our various expeditions on E 19. Here,
so close to Chinook, we were allowed to explore on our own. On one
hike across the island Pete instructed me about rattlesnake bites, as
I mentioned earlier. And then there is the famous egg story! I am not
sure what year it was, nor am I sure what year I set down the
episode in an essay. Certainly my account was written while I was
still in elementary school (no later than 1942) and I offer it here in its
original form, but with the many, many spelling corrections by Aunt
Gladys. The essay bears the title, "The Joy of Camping."

> One morning when we were in Canada Pete and I planned a camp-
> ing trip. We packed some food in the knapsack but we didn't take
> any water because the water in Georgian Bay is pure. As soon as

we had landed on E 19 we started going inland. We had almost reached the middle of the island when it was time for lunch. Pete decided to boil his egg so he put it in the skillet without water and put it on the fire and waited expectantly. Suddenly the unexpected happened. The egg exploded much to his disappointment. It was the best scrambled egg he had ever eaten he declared afterwards.

Soon we arrived at the prearranged spot and set up a tent with much difficulty. When night arrived we both settled in to bed. We were up most that night killing mosquitoes.

Toward morning we dropped off to sleep. Suddenly without warning the tent collapsed. We crawled out and discovered it was six o'clock. Since we couldn't sleep we decided to get breakfast but some animal had nibbled all the bacon and fish we had. So we ate applesauce that morning. I had had all I could stand so I went home for another breakfast and Pete went home to sleep.

Looking back I seem to recall that my egg was broken before we ever reached the spot where we had lunch. I had put the egg loose in my knapsack, but, at some point on our hike, I had the misfortune of falling backward onto the knapsack, smashing the egg.

All of us, I'm sure, can no longer be certain of the precise year of some of the events we remember. Probably this story of our camping trip merges two different occasions. Pete has some other memories of those years 1935-1940:

Dr. Pope gave me for my tenth birthday the 10 rattles from a rattlesnake he had killed.

The only time I remember my dad coming up to the island, Dix and I took him fishing. We wished him good luck because we could catch fish anytime. He proceeded to catch all the fish.

The summer of 1941, with war already underway for so many, was the last of these "typical" summers, as it was to become the last summer of innocence for the United States. My brothers and cousins were not to return to our islands for several years. Betsy Read spent five days on her family's island, Peace, that summer with the young man, Henry Holt, who was to become her husband. After an absence of sixty years she returned to see that island once again!

By 1941 the original cottage on E 3 had been much expanded. I spent a month there with Aunt Gladys after my parents departed. It was a cold summer and I had my cot on the porch right against the stones of the fireplace. They seemed to share some stored heat with me in the night. The "big" boys were now grown, some married, and life seemed quieter that summer. Pete and I were busy, however, attempting for some reason to build a hut. We chopped down many small cedars, much to the disgust of a teacher friend visiting Aunt Gladys, and built a most unsatisfactory structure behind the cottage on E 3. That was the last summer at the island for my family until 1944. But the McDonalds managed to come up the following summer and hut building continued (more successfully), as Pete informs us:

> The summer of 1942, I built a tree house (on E 9), just behind Chinook. It was made from small arborvitae cut below and birch bark walls and roof from Shawanaga Island Birch Grove. I think it has one million nails in it. I even made a wooden lock with a latch string. The first night completed, I slept in it as a test.

In 1943, as mentioned, Carrie Bartow records that she was the only one up for the summer.

In February, 1944, I wrote in a letter to my Aunt Gwen that we had heard from Ethel Williams and that she planned on going to her island the following August. She hoped that we would be able to make the trip as well. That June I had both feet operated on and, as a recompense for my pain and suffering, my parents agreed to attempt a brief visit to the island in August. Before they closed the cottage on Eagle in 1941 the big boys had the strength to heave a large old sailboat with a heavy metal centerboard into the living room. In 1944 there was no one able to lift it out again. Since that cottage was unusable, we stayed on E 3. The major challenge to our trip was rationing, particularly gasoline rationing. I do not know how my father managed to get ration coupons for enough gas to get us from St. Louis to the border and back, but he did. Securing the necessary coupons for gasoline in Canada was more difficult. Since he could claim with justification that we depended upon our little outboard to ferry us to the store for groceries, he was given a large number of coupons for outboard motor fuel. When we were ready to depart Mr. Woodward had Dad back the car up to the pump on the dock where the marine fuel was dispensed and he filled up the tank, accepting the boat coupons. Probably that one tank would have gotten us across the border, but my father began to worry. Finally in some town in southern Ontario he pulled into a gasoline station and managed to talk the woman there into giving us a few extra gallons without any coupons at all!

At the border we encountered another problem with rationing. This time it was the coupons for food. Sugar, coffee, meat, cheese, fats, fish and canned goods, including jam, were all rationed by this time. In the U.S. where each person had a monthly number of ration stamps, one was issued 16 stamps a week for all meat, cheese, and shortening and one pound of cheese required 8 of the 16. I do not remember the rationing system used in Canada, but I recall it was strict on the sugar, but much more generous on the meat and cheese. At any rate my mother had been able to buy several pounds of Canadian cheese and she proposed to take it home with us. At the U.S. border, however, the customs officials demanded that she surrender U.S. stamps for the cheese. She was outraged because, as she said, bringing in cheese did not deprive anyone in the U.S. of his or her allotted ration! In the end she told the officers to keep the cheese and hurl it into the river! Who knows what happened to it?

Rationing was still in effect in 1945, the last summer of the war, but I do not remember that it caused us any difficulty. Almost every cottager old or young enough not to be engaged in the war effort managed a visit that summer. The end of the war was in sight. Germany had surrendered, but Japan fought on. We were back on E 3, the boat still in the cottage on Eagle. My parents slept in the bunk house there and paddled up to E 3 each morning before breakfast. I remember that our family was worried that Bob Donovan, who had been stationed in Europe, might be sent to the Pacific theater. We knew that Dick Donovan had been engaged in war work at a place called Oak Ridge, although we had no idea of what was involved until after the bombs fell that August. By the end of that summer one epoch had ended and a new one begun, for our cottage community and for our world.

7:60. The Catboat with Gladys Dickey aboard 1946

CHAPTER SEVEN

Changes After the War, 1946 - 1962

The limits for this next period in our story are difficult to fix. Its start in 1946, the first full summer after the war, is easily identified, but it is much more difficult to find a specific year for the end. One could, I suppose, end with the deaths of many of that first generation. Helen Whitelaw died on January 19, 1962 and Lucy Young died the same month. My father died on April 15, 1965 and Chet Bartow, Sr. died December 19 of the same year. Those first five years of the 1960s mark endings and beginnings as the following accounts will make clear. The most appropriate year for an ending is, however, 1962, for that year was the last in which we had to go out around Carolyn to reach our islands. By the following year we could go behind Carolyn instead, but that story belongs in the next chapter!

Personally I can divide this period into two. First, starting when I was 16 in 1946, and ending when I graduated from college in 1951, I enjoyed an unbroken series of carefree summers. But in the second, most of the 1950s, adulthood and its responsibilities called both Pete and me away and our knowledge of those summers comes from others. This is a common pattern, childhood and teenage years spent at the cottage followed by an absence of some years before a return with a young family of one's own. During the second half of this period the older members of our second generation initiated the pattern. It was a time of construction of new cottages and the repair and expansion of old ones.

Before returning to spend the summer in 1946 my parents had the old sailboat removed from our cottage, had a fireplace built, a bedroom and washroom added, and the porch extended. When my father learned that asbestos shingles never needed painting, he decided to have the entire cottage shingled in white, a decision we were one day to regret. This summer turned out to be an eventful one. My brother Bob begins the story:

> The summer of 1946, when I was newly discharged from the army, Hope came to the Island for the first time. We came from St. Louis the old fashioned way, by train, and I remember that Aunt Gladys, fearing that Hope had been painted too rosy a picture of island life, began to dwell on its inconveniences and drawbacks. She mentioned Kennedy's and pine beetles and kerosene stoves and outhouses, but Hope was not deterred, and in fact she turned out to be a true Georgian Bay islander, taking everything in stride and learning to cope with Kennedy's, pine beetles, kerosene stoves, and outhouses. Her only complaint, really, was that in the absence of full-length mirrors and bathroom scales, somehow the dress she had worn for the trip up in June did not fit quite so well for the trip back in September. She says she has never been the same since.

> Of all the events of that long and active summer, one in particular stands out in my memory. All during the summer the family expanded and contracted as some arrived and others departed, but five of us were there for the entire summer, from late June until early September: Aunt Gladys, Bill, Betsy, Hope, and I. Bill and Hope and I took it into our heads to go in to the Station one day, not in itself a difficult or perilous enterprise, but we elected to go in the ancient catboat (of which the mast still survives on the rafters of the house on Eagle Island), which we brought

around to the front dock the evening before (fig. 7:60). Betsy, who was only nine, was not to be allowed to go, though she complained bitterly at being excluded. When Hope and I came up to the main cottage from the bunk house next morning, Betsy greeted us triumphantly, jumping up and down in glee.

"The catboat's sunk! The catboat's sunk!"

It was a fact. The painter, still tied to a dock ring, was apparently the only thing keeping the boat from slipping to the bottom of French's Bay. But we were young enough, and foolish enough, to persist in our plan, so we hauled the boat up and bailed it out with a bucket until it floated again, and we were able to sustain the illusion that we had a seaworthy craft. The three of us set out for the Station by way of Shawanaga Bay. Hope spent the entire trip bailing in order to keep us afloat while Bill and I attended to the business of sailing the boat.

The reason why we felt it imperative to go to the Station has gone from my memory, but I do remember that we went into Kennedy's and bought, among other things, a new axe. At this distance it hardly seems sufficient justification for the ordeal. At any rate, when we got back to the boat the gunwales were awash, and it took prompt action to keep the craft afloat. Somehow we managed to get back home again, but Hope again had to bail the whole way. Her impression of the entire trip is limited to the sloshing bilge that she had to contend with.

I, too, well remember that trip, although I recall sharing the bailing with Hope. At the end of that summer, feeling that the catboat was not worth the cost of storage, we dragged it up on the shore. When we returned the next year it had disappeared, never to be seen again. Perhaps it finally found the bottom of French's Bay! Presumably we purchased some groceries that day at Kennedy's, but it was on weekly trips to the Ojibway that we purchased almost all of our food. In one letter home I remarked, "Dr. Pope came for dinner and for once the Ojibway had fresh vegetables, so we had sirloin steak and corn on the cob." Bob reminds us that the effects of the war were still to be felt in food preparation that summer:

Most grocery shopping was done at the Ojibway, which still maintained an old-fashioned butcher shop, but in those days right after the war, not all foods were in plentiful supply, and sugar was still rationed. It was a bit disturbing to find that a can of peaches might require one person's entire monthly sugar ration. Under the circumstances, we made what use we could of liquid saccharine as a sweetener, but Hope found out to her dismay that a little too much saccharine turns food bitter. It was particularly distressing that she made the discovery with some stewed blueberries that we had spent the morning picking.

In still another letter I commented on an additional service provided that summer which I do not remember being repeated: "Bob got a haircut because the Ojibway now keeps a barber on Tuesdays and Thursdays who sets up shop in a shed. He is very slow but very good. (He runs a hairdressing place in Toronto and is doing this for the summer to help out because he is on vacation.)"

I have many memories of that summer kept alive in this series of letters that formed a diary mailed to my parents in St. Louis. My father had only four weeks of vacation, so he, my mother, and sister Didge who wanted the experience of being an "only child" had departed from the island by the end of July. The first entry is dated July 28th. To understand what follows one needs to know that, as an infant, I called Aunt Gladys "Da," a name we all continued to use. It is also necessary to know that all her life she was always the first to take on any chore, the first to leap up from the table to clear and wash the dishes. Every summer we had a rota for chores and, being lazy sixteen, I frequently avoided my turn simply by claiming to be tired. I knew Aunt Gladys would always step in to do my work. This particular misadventure began as Bob and I tried to rig a canoe for sailing:

Finally we were fixed to go sailing, so when I got back from Da's (E 3), Bob asked me to go with him and try (the canoe) out, so off we went. (I had left my shoes, socks, and glasses behind as quite a wind was blowing.) As soon as we were out in French's Bay Bob decided to sail down to Leonard's to see if we had it rigged right (we hadn't). After leaving his place we tried to sail home but, because the leeboard was in the wrong place, Bob had to paddle some of the way. When we got home we were in a pretty pickle. It seems that Hope had finished preparing supper just as we set sail, so she was VERY mad at us. So mad in fact that this is what she said (I had made the remark that we would eat the dinner whether it was cold or not),

"You bet you'll eat it, every scrap, and you and Bob will also scrape, wash, dry and put away the dishes!"

(The last almost in tears) After this outburst we had a very glum supper to be sure (especially me when I heard I had to do the dishes). Finally (after dessert) Da said, "Well, Bill and I will do the dishes." Then Hope said, "No, Bill and I'll do them." Then Bob said, "Bill and I will do them." Then Da said, "No, Bill and Betsy will do them." So we did while Bob and Hope went for a sail. After we finished Betsy and I went for a sail and then we had a game of chess and so to bed.

After more than fifty years since that summer I look back with astonishment at Hope's ability to cope with a new environment, an extended family, and all that she was asked to do. Not least do I marvel that she and Bob were so willing to have a younger brother tag along on so many expeditions. One example from my diary letters describes a trip to the McCoys after which Hope always said that in future she wanted a boat "with high sides!"

Thursday, August 1

It was such a nice day today Bob, Hope, and I decided to make some sandwiches and go off for a day's trip. We started off in the green canoe for Hole-in-the-Wall but decided to go to the McCoys when we got out to the end of Mud Channel. We went to the little McCoy, but just as we got there the wind changed to the west and we decided we had better just take a walk and then go home. So, we ate after a little walk during which Hope decided she wanted to buy the island. We started home about two and such waves you have never seen. Hope lay on the bottom of the canoe while Bob and I paddled. Almost every wave broke into the canoe and by the time we got back (about 3:30) Hope had changed her mind about wanting to buy the McCoys.

We did not often attend the annual regatta of the Pointe au Baril Islanders' Association, but we did in 1946. I described a major expedition for which Archie Taylor's water taxi was engaged for the day (I suspect paid for by Aunt Gladys). The day following we had a more typical event, a community picnic:

Saturday, August 3

Mrs. Taylor called for us as was arranged and I was delegated to ride in the rowboat towed behind. It was very thrilling because the boat would swerve from side to side and this caused the bow to almost go under every second.

We had a good dinner at the Ojibway and saw the first few canoe races. Betsy was just wild to enter the race for girls under 10 in freestyle swimming but she had forgotten her bathing suit so she couldn't.

Then we went on up to the Village. On the way we saw this huge yacht which had run on a rock and bent its propeller shaft and thus it was waiting for a tug to take it to Meaford. After visits to the lighthouse and to Richardson's we went back to the Ojibway so Betsy could use the (flush) toilet...and then we came home.

Sunday, August 4

We spent the day resting from Saturday. Da had ordered 3 dozen hot dogs for a supper picnic. So this afternoon we spent in getting ready. Bob made the fire and I cut toasting sticks. The Popes, Rileys, and the Whitelaws were the guests and you should have seen the time we had loading and unloading the boats! Dr. Pope took the record, eating six hot dogs and I came in second with 5. Bob and Hope tied for third with 4. All the guests left early.

On Wednesday, August 7, Mrs. Riley drowned. This was the first, and so far only, death to occur during the summer in our small island community. While it made a great impression upon me, it all happened so suddenly and I was so caught up as a participant in the events of that afternoon that I did not feel the full implications of such a tragic event. My account in the following letter omits some of the details. That afternoon Helen Grove's brother, Leo

Lewandowski, and his family arrived to occupy the Grove cottage. Archie Taylor brought them and as he passed from Mud Channel, between Popes' and Rileys,' he saw Mr. Riley waving to him. It seems that Mr. Riley had been off in his rowboat and when he returned to his island he found his wife's body floating near the shore.

> Bob, Hope, and Betsy spent the morning fishing and I read (Fortitude). Then this afternoon, as I was reading, Archie Taylor drove up with his boat rattling to beat the band. It seems the towrope which he had used to bring the Groves' boat down had gotten snarled around the propeller. I had to dive down with a knife to cut it loose while Da and Bob hurried over to the Rileys' because Taylor said that Mrs. Riley had drowned. I went over with him after cutting away the rope and found Mr. Lewandowski and Bob giving artificial respiration. I hurried back to the Groves' to take the shutters off so Leo's wife and kids could get into the cottage. Taylor went to the Ojibway for the doctor. He returned just as I came back from working on the cottage. The doctor said that she was dead, so they carried her up to the cottage. Da stayed to help Mr. Riley pack, while we went home. Then, after supper, Mr. Richardson himself came back in his big boat with the undertaker and the police. The Popes took Mr. Riley up to the Station, while Richardson followed with the body. They were first going to take Mr. Riley to Parry Sound on his way home.
>
> Da and I have to go over and help close his cottage tomorrow.
>
> P.S. Mr. Riley found her in water only knee deep, so she must have fainted.

After the tragedy on the day they arrived, the Lewandowski family settled into the Grove cottage. Bob and Hope must have been relieved because they were liberated from my almost constant company by my interest in this new family. Mr. Lewandowski introduced me to fishing from a motor boat and, once started, I continued to use such a boat for trolling until I grew sick of the noise and smell from the motor many years later. He also taught me to use the lure, Johnson Silver Minnow, with a bit of red rubber in place of the recommended pork rind. I have long wondered if a pike, having once tasted rubber rather than delicious rind, would ever strike at the lure a second time? My diary letter explained:

> Wednesday, August 14
>
> Neither Mrs. Lewandowski nor the children can swim, so they won't go to the Ojibway with Leo nor will they go any place in the boat. Therefore, I do everything with him. I am going to the Ojibway today with him and I have been fishing with him almost every day. Mr. Lewandowski won't touch fish and neither will the children, so only Mrs. L. eats the fish he catches. He does not like to fish for small fish, so we spend our time after pike. He uses the motor in trolling, so it is not so much work for me, but he goes so fast that at first I didn't think he would catch anything. Sunday, however, he caught a 6 pound pike in the little bay back of the "Bass Hole" and I caught a 5 pound one in the entrance to the same bay. We put both of them in our live-box and they both managed to squeeze out.

In 1946 my father bought our first boat actually designed for an outboard motor, a Peterborough "Speedster." This boat was recommended for five to six persons and for motors up to eighteen h.p.; we had a two and one half h.p.! In the following years he bought a Lawson motor (six h.p.) and, finally, in the 1950s a Johnson ten h.p. The graceful boat's beautiful varnish was, late in our ownership, overlaid with green and orange paint. By this time Didge had decided to name our boat the Cruddy Sark! Handsome or not, it provided excellent service for more than 30 years and ended its days powered by an Evinrude nine point nine h.p.

At this time we also welcomed new families who were joining our community. Jean Hofmann tells the story of the first of them:

> The Foutz family first arrived on Mud Channel through the hospitality of Helen Grove. Soon after the end of World War II, Gertrude Foutz (my Aunt Dickie) was invited to join the Groves during their summer stay at their island. While there, Aunt Dickie spoke of her nieces, the youngest of whom was the same age as Helen Grove's daughter, Nancy.
>
> Aunt Dickie's next invitation to Groves' island was extended to

include that niece. Thus it was that in 1947, at the age of 14, I first saw Georgian Bay.

The Groves were gracious hosts who provided me with a truly delightful experience. Nancy and Judy Grove and I became instant friends, and we giggled and chattered for two weeks as only adolescent girls do. Now Nancy and I share a dear red-haired grandson, Lonnie Ray Hofmann, whose father is my older son, Steve, and whose mother is Nancy's oldest daughter, Wendy. (Steve and Wendy were married in 1981—an island romance that "took.")

On returning home to Ohio, I regaled my family with endless tales of the beauty and magic of Georgian Bay, where a sunset can be as spectacular as a fireworks display, while the stillness of a misty morning can seem to be an almost sacred experience. I didn't realize at the time that I was actually giving my parents a sales pitch.

The following spring, Aunt Dickie wrote in a postscript to one of her weekly letters to our family: "Helen Grove tells me that Ethel (Williams) Plimpton has decided to sell her island." Within hours my father had telephoned Aunt Dickie and asked her to find out how he could contact Ethel Plimpton. Calls and letters went back and forth, and in what now seems like an incredibly brief period of time, Ralph and Dorothy Foutz had purchased Chinook, sight unseen. (The title transfer was complete on June 11, 1948.)

One of my letters from that summer survives. In it I tell my parents about my trip from St. Louis to Pointe au Baril with Aunt Gladys and my sisters, Didge and Betsy, and about opening the cottage. Some details may be of interest, especially the prices!

...we ate lunch in Marshall, Michigan and finally reached Port Huron about 6:52 p.m. after having played tag with trucks all day. Da was in a hurry and, since we had had what some might call a dinner in Marshall, she induced us to eat a pickup supper in a drug store. I had two putrid ham sandwiches, a glass of milk, and some ice cream for $0.80. We drove on to the border where Da told the immigration officer that she was born in "Iowa, Iowa."...We arrived in Grand Bend, Ontario (on highway

21) about 9:05 p.m....We finally arrived at Westlake's (Tourist Home) about 9:30 p.m., 14 miles north of Grand Bend. Their bathroom was fixed and we had good beds and a good breakfast for $6....

We arrived at the Island yesterday (July 3) noon and found ourselves locked out. The girls and I paddled over to Helen Whitelaw's to get the key. The house was very clean, only one mouse (dead). There was quite a bit of fresh gnawing, however...Gordon Smith brought us out and he told us that Mr. Richardson is working this summer as a helper until the new owner (Groskorth) learns the ropes. Mrs. Richardson is no longer here but is expected to come up for a couple of weeks....

This morning we found some animal lodged just above the damper in the fireplace. We opened it and I looked up with a flashlight and saw some bird trying to fly up the chimney. We worked for a couple of hours trying to get it down. Finally I opened the damper and we left to go swimming. While we were eating dinner it came down through the fireplace and made its way into the tool closet. The bird turned out to be a duck. Da got it out the back door and it flew off toward Big Island.

An unusual accident marked the end of the 1940s. Our family physician and friend, Ted Jean, and family visited us in August, 1949. Ted had flown up in his small airplane and landed at the airport in Gravenhurst. Although I no longer remember the reason, it was decided that I would join him on the return flight to St. Louis. He had decided to fly north over our islands and to clear with Canadian authorities, landing at an airport marked on the charts at Little Current on Manitoulin Island. From there he expected to fly across the Upper Peninsula of Michigan before heading south. The day we departed was clear but a very strong northwest wind was blowing. For the first time I had a chance to see our islands from the air that afternoon. We flew over our island and I was impressed by the way in which underwater shoals were clearly visible from that height. As we passed over the Lighthouse I was at the controls and became very alarmed when the plane suddenly dove and wobbled. It took me a moment to realize that Ted was responsible—he had spotted Archie Taylor below and was wagging the wings in greeting!

Our flight ended unexpectedly and abruptly, however, when we landed at Little Current. Ted, fearing that the high wind might flip the plane, decided to land directly into it despite the fact that this course would require crossing the runway at an angle. The grass covered terrain below us disguised a ditch at the edge of the runway. We touched down safely, but when we reached the ditch the plane nosed in and ended with the landing gear crushed and the tail high in the air. Outside of a minor cut or two we were unharmed. We were alone at the airfield except for a boy watching some cows; he came over to see what had happened.

We spent the night in a hotel in Little Current and the next day Ted chartered a bush pilot to fly us in his float plane down to Windsor from whence we crossed over to Detroit to catch a commercial flight to St. Louis. Fortunately classes for my Junior year at Washington University were not scheduled to start for a few weeks, so I returned to Little Current with a friend to retrieve the plane. We drove Ted's big Chrysler towing a trailer designed to hold an airplane with its wings detached and mounted lengthwise on either side. The trip was made more difficult because Highway 17 was under construction with a gravel surface the entire distance. The greatest difficulty, however, was to disassemble the aircraft. Neither of us knew how to do it, having had only a few minutes of instruction from the mechanic in St. Louis. The bush pilots, who were supposed to help, did not appear until it was time to lift the fuselage onto the trailer. Before that we had had to siphon gasoline from the wing tanks. We made little progress with the disassembly until we finally borrowed a set of socket wrenches from a local garage. With the proper tools we completed the job at last and returned the plane to Ted who had it repaired and took it into the air once more.

The 1950s began with almost a "rite of passage," a canoe trip to the French River! I had heard about the expedition my brothers and the Erdmann boys had made years before and felt that I, too, must go there. During the summer, 1950, Pete McDonald, Dave Robertson (a friend of the Groves) and I made the trip. The three of us crammed all our gear into the ancient green Peterborough canoe (sixteen feet long). We took turns paddling, while the one who sat in the bottom kept a line out for fish. I remember we caught quite a few bass and even had several on the stringer on our return. We were the

ones, however, who were truly caught, caught by our lack of experience and proper gear. We discovered how difficult it is to sleep on
Georgian Bay rocks with only a few blankets or a thin sleeping bag.
We discovered that it is almost impossible to camp without a tent or
netting to keep mosquitoes at bay. We discovered that the sun can
burn terribly, despite protective clothing, when one is out on the
water all day. And we discovered that any canoe trip requires proper charts.

Because of the mosquitoes we were forced to find shelter
each night, in an abandoned hut the first and third nights and in the
base of a range light at the mouth of the French River on the second.
We did not sleep well the entire trip! All of us suffered from the sun.
A hat did not prevent the sun from burning the tops of my ears,
while poor Dave Robertson's lips burned and cracked. Pete and I,
I'm afraid, were not very helpful, telling jokes to make him laugh
when every movement of his lips was agony. Without charts except
for one general map we were never sure of our location, but, keeping the open water to our left and islands to our right as we went
north, we knew we were going in the right direction and we did end
up at, what appeared to be, the mouth of a river that, to us, will
always be the French River!

Back on our islands cottage life continued as usual. Another
memory I have of those years is discovering an exotic new dish,
pizza! Dorothy Foutz introduced this treat when we gathered to
swim at Chinook. She had difficulty keeping up with demand!

In 1951 I graduated from university and that was the last full
summer I spent at the island for many years. In 1952 I took a job
teaching sailing at a camp for boys in northern Wisconsin and that
summer, and for the following two, I managed only a few days' visit
late in August. My family wrote to me at camp that the water level
was quite high in 1952. It was so high that my father estimated that
another 3 feet and our cottage would be flooded! The next year
Helen Whitelaw, suffering from acute depression, decided suddenly
to sell her island. Her decision was made so quickly and she departed so abruptly that she left behind a house guest, Nell Milam. My
mother took her in until her return trip could be arranged. Jean
Hofmann recalls how her father, learning of Helen's decision to sell
E 5, decided to purchase it:

For several years (beginning in 1948) my parents, my sister Helen ("Tiny") and I, as well as my friend Annie Briihl, enjoyed our summer holidays on Chinook.

While in residence on Mud Channel in 1953, my father went to the Ojibway to purchase supplies and happened to see a notice on the dockside bulletin board. Dated that same day, the notice offered Helen Whitelaw's island for sale and listed a number to call if one were interested. Once again, fortuitous timing smiled upon him—he made a phone call from the dock and set in motion the purchase of E 5.

My mother preferred the cottage on E 5 to the one on Chinook, and so all of their subsequent visits to the bay were spent on Kingbird, the name they chose for the island.

Jean's sister Molly, married to Jim Franklin, also remembers their early years:

We came with the rest of the Foutz family in 1952. Linda was 3 1/2 and Mike 2 1/2. They fished off the old high dock with 10-cent-store poles and caught pan fish and watched blue-eyed baby catfish and as a family we were committed to E 18. We came back each year until Jim was unable to make the trip.

When Dad bought E 5, the whole group transferred there and Chinook remained boarded up until sometime in the mid to late 1960s. Jim and I spent much of one week dislodging bats and mice, washing down walls with bleach and planning to move in the following summer. Thereafter both islands were in use each year.

When Jim retired from IBM at 55, we began to come for two months each summer and took on bigger projects, the most memorable probably being the year the entire extended Franklin clan arrived. We tore down part of the leaking chimney and, with a hole in the roof, endured a three day blow.

Jim and the boys, often with friends, came up in May several times, but the rest of us opted for blueberry and swimming weather.

After we deeded the island to our children, when the added-on-kitchen became a precarious attachment, an addition to the cottage added a bigger kitchen, bath and bedroom. Since then the younger Franklins have spent more time and effort.

For three years (1952-1954) I managed a few days at the island   at the end of the summer after camp was over. For the remainder of the decade I did not get back because I was fully occupied studying and excavating in Greece and getting established at Florida State University in my first teaching position. At last I returned for a short visit to Georgian Bay in 1960. My brother Bob, however, remembers his summers there during those years during the 1950s:

> It was five years (after 1946) before we were able to get to the Island again, in the summer of 1951, when Faith was two. We had moved back to St. Louis, and again we came by train, which was quite a thrill for Faith, who shared a lower berth with Hope, while I slept (a part of the night, anyway) in the upper.
>
> That summer our front dock was bolted to the rock, near the water pipe, and Faith used to have her bath right on the dock in two inches of sun-warmed water in the old galvanized baby bathtub. I don't think Hope and I would have been able to do very much that summer, with a two-year old to look after, but Betsy frequently came to our rescue. Every morning after breakfast Faith would say brightly "Let's play blocks!" or "Let's go draw!" and Betsy would always respond. Once when Hope and I were out somewhere in a boat, Faith fell into the water from the front dock, and Betsy dived in after her without a moment's hesitation.
>
> Bill and I were sleeping in the bunk house that summer, while Faith and the ladies slept in the main cottage. One night a storm came up, with a strong east wind and a driving rain, but Bill and I slept right through it in the relatively sheltered bunk house. The people in the main cottage, however, were kept awake, listening anxiously to the buffeting of the motor boat, moored at the exposed front dock. At length the situation became desperate when the boat threatened to tear loose from its mooring, but Bill

and I slept blissfully on. The first we knew of the emergency was when Mother came running barefoot to the bunk house, dressed only in her nightgown. We got the situation under control, but I shall always remember tiny little Faith, her nightie flapping in the wind, watching us cope with the storm.

These were difficult years for us, and it was not always possible to indulge in the luxury of an island summer. I spent one summer as a carhop at the Parkmoor in St. Louis and another selling toys for a wholesale jobber, and of course it was during these years that Peter was born. It was 1954 when we next managed to come up, and again we had a two-year old. We lived in Ithaca now, and made the trip in our old 1946 Dodge.

I remember the evening we arrived at the Island. We were gathered round the supper table, exchanging news with other members of the family we had not seen for over a year. No one was paying any attention to Peter, who could not break into the conversation to make his wants known, so he simply got out of his high chair and crawled across the table for a second piece of cornbread.

Both the children took to the Island, and though Faith was not yet swimming she enjoyed going into the water, and Peter was always part fish, though his little body was so solid and chunky that he didn't seem to have the natural buoyancy most children have. He has not been able to float to this day.

Bob's story is interrupted at this point because there was a gap of several years before they returned for another summer. But while I was in Greece letters from my family in Georgian Bay in 1955 mentioned propane stoves and fridges and George Erdmann's Snipe, the first of his many sailboats. In 1956 I learned from family letters that Pete and Nancy McDonald were visiting and that George and Sue Erdmann were looking for an island to purchase. George tells the story:

During the middle 50s Sue and I began to think of getting a place of our own in Georgian Bay. It was getting to be a problem to arrange just when we could have some time at E 3 and when we were there with Mother and Dad it was a bit crowded. I had always been quite lucky in my commanding officers in the army and was usually able to get them to OK my summer leave when I wanted it. But it would be nice to have our own cottage and little kingdom on an island. Naturally we wanted to stay in the Mud Channel area where all of our friends were so we started our search in that place. We looked at sections of E 1 and a point of Big Island just opposite E 3. We even thought about what was not much more than a large shoal, E 4, just off of E 1. We thought about E 19 but really wanted a smaller island rather than a piece of a large one. I don't know if either E 19 or Big Island could have been purchased a little bit at a time. B 934, just to the NE of Eagle, had some possibilities but again it was a larger island. We canoed on down to Frederic Inlet but we were not thrilled about being that far away. I'm sure that we looked at several other islands during this period but can't remember their numbers or the geography.

One day we were paddling slowly back from wandering over the small island in Groves Channel, B 986, when we met Ben who was out for a paddle in ME. We were talking over our frustrations when she mentioned that she had heard that Eleanor Read might be interested in selling their island, E 27. We had not even considered it since it was already patented. Reuben and Eleanor Read and their daughter Betsy had owned E 27 since 1932. They did believe in really roughing it; their cottage was just four walls with a roof and without a floor except for the nice smooth rock. It had big barn type doors in both ends and the building was really just to store their gear in during the winter or in inclement weather. They usually slept in hammocks slung between trees and cooked on an open fire place they built to the southeast of the cottage. During the war Reuben Read had died from complications of appendicitis and, to the best of my knowledge, Eleanor and Betsy had not been up since that time.

Summer was about over by this time, at least ours was, so we had to leave for our long drive back to Fort Lewis in the state of Washington. Needless to say, just as soon as we arrived there I put in a telephone call to Mrs. Read to ask about her plans and to put in my bid for first refusal. Sue and I had looked over the cottage and contents (it was not difficult to get into any cottage in the bay) and it had virtually nothing in it, no boats, no cooking

7.61. The Erdmann prefab on E 27 in 1957.

utensils other than a rusty frypan, and a few pieces of rotted cloth of unknown use. I'm sure that Mrs. Read didn't believe our report of the condition of the cottage and held off giving us an answer until she could contact Helen Whitelaw to ask her about the status. Helen had to agree with us and the final result was that we were offered the island at a reasonable price. We were delighted to say the least.

The following summer, 1957, was a busy one and there are two accounts of it. First, George continues by describing the construction of a new cottage on E 27:

The fall and winter of 1956-1957 was spent studying plans from a host of pre-fab builders. I had been sent to Washington, D.C. to take an advanced course in dentistry and when not studying hard I poured over the catalogs. I don't know why I spent so much time looking at all the offerings in the book, since it was most obvious that we could only afford the least expensive and smallest. Selection made, we ordered and then wrote to Jerry Evoy that it was coming and to please get the parts out to the island. I wanted to have it all ready for our arrival when we would camp out on the island while putting the pre-fab together. Jerry did get the pieces to the island and, after seeing the size of them, I wonder to this day just how he managed to get them ashore. No damage was done except for a small crack in one pane of glass, so insignificant that the crack is still there. Mother and Dad were vacationing on E 3 at this time and when they saw the size of the pieces they took it upon themselves to arrange to have John Hodgson put three men for three days on the project to do what they could. When we finally arrived the cottage was erected and the roof mostly on. I had only to finish the roof and build a temporary set of steps to be able to reach the front door and we were able to move in (fig. 7:61).

During the previous winter a strong wind had blown open the west doors of the old Read cottage, then lifted the entire cottage and flung it against the fireplace, doing no good to either. After finishing the work on our new cottage I began to demolish the old, trying to salvage what I could. The roof sheathing, the rafters and the studding were all that could be used, the rest only good for many years of marshmallow roast parties on the wind-swept outer part of E 27. Our new cottage was beastly hot that summer, so arranged for John Hodgson to put a porch on part of the front and the east wall, using what he could of the salvaged lumber from the Read cottage and so we maintained a bit of continuity with the old.

That same summer Gladys Dickey kept a log which she entitled "One August in Georgian Bay: A Memoir." She made copies for all nieces, nephews, grandnieces and grandnephews who were there that month and they were a legion! Their number included Jim Erdmann, his wife Jean and children Johnny, Ellen, Nancy, and Margaret. They arrived August 4 and there were nine who sat down to dinner that night on E 3! George and Sue moved right into their new cottage on arrival, August 15, with their three, Molly, Gwen, and David bringing the total up to thirteen Erdmanns for dinner over on E 3 that night! My brother Dick and his sons Mike and Steve together with my sister Betsy made up the Donovan contingent, arriving after a two-day drive from St. Louis in the evening of August 12. Gladys' account of those last two weeks reminds us of the great labor involved in feeding a large extended family from a little cottage kitchen. Fortunately for them there was no prejudice against food from cans! Typically Aunt Gladys makes deprecating remarks about her own cooking ("made some miserable icing," e.g.). Her entries for August 16 and for August 22 provide samples:

> Everybody was to come here (B 980) to swim today. So, I spent the morning making spice cake, brownies and cinnamon rolls out of Bisquick.
>
> Dinner was easy as I had spaghetti and cold ham; gingerbread with lemon sauce for dessert. Betsy had baked the ham with a delicious orange sauce.
>
> After dinner I fixed the milk for the cocoa, and set the table for high tea, making sandwiches and fixing crackers and cheese.
>
> Clint, Jr. (Grove) and Steve (Malone) arrived early and by four all were present, including Belinda and Angela (the pets). Gwen rowed down by herself later.
>
> By five they were all reluctantly dragged from the water, and we all finally assembled on the porch. The little girls slid in on the bench next to Mike and David, and Margaret occupied the end. How they did enjoy the food! I don 't know what we would have done if the Groves had come! Gwen decided to bring her party down here Sunday—as there is more room.
>
> August 22:...I took the first step toward a picnic lunch by making a pan of fudge and putting it on the table to cool. Just then Jim, Jean and Margaret appeared and sampled it. Then George's three appeared. In a trice it was gone. Little Gwen said she had had nine pieces, but I don't know whether she was the champion or not.
>
> Dick and George went off to the McCoys alone, so the children were all here for lunch. Betsy made sandwiches and we each had half a banana for dessert...Later they played bridge while David napped. At three they all set out for Gwen's island (E 3) to swim.
>
> At six they returned—and Helen Grove arrived with pike chowder and delicious hot rolls. I had cabbage and pineapple salad, spaghetti for Mike and Steve, and cottage pudding—the nastiest I have ever tasted....

7.62. Gladys Dickey celebrates a birthday in her cottage on E 3,
(l. to r.), John E. Donovan, Gladys, her sister Gwen Erdmann, her grandneice,
also Gwen Erdmann, her sister Dorothy Donovan, late 1950s

In her chronicle of that summer Aunt Gladys provides a brief glimpse of the construction of the new cottage on E 27 (which she always calls "Peace," the name given to the island by the Reads). Evoy delivered the material for the cottage on Friday, August 2, and she describes going over

> ...after supper...to Peace to survey the pre-fab. It looked like enough lumber for a three bed-room house. But it did seem too big a job for one or two amateurs. So Gwen and Morris decided to write Hodgson to go ahead. The side walls will take four men to lift in place.

The letter must have been delivered with lightening speed, for by Monday, August 5, she reports

> ...hearing hammering from George's island, so Mr. Hodgson must be there.

The next day she visited the site and found the walls up.

She comments that

> it seems like a shell, but none of us want anything too civilized.
> George expects to add a porch later.

Finally she tells us that the roof was to go on the following day (Wednesday, August 7). It was indeed speedy construction for a cottage in our area, delivery of material on August 2 to occupancy of the finished cottage thirteen days later! The "house warming" was held on a rainy evening, August 24, to which Aunt Gladys took another pan of fudge together with crackers to scoop it up with as it had not gotten firm. The entire crowd managed to fit inside.

The entry in the diary for August 19 deserves to be quoted as does that for August 20 on which date Aunt Gladys celebrated her 69th birthday (fortunate are those with summer birthdays to be celebrated at the island, fig. 7:62). Both entries illustrate very well the fun so characteristic of summer life in our islands.

> August 19: Jim came by with a canoe load for an overnight hike on Big Island. We watched them land there. And Dick, Betsy and Mike and Steve hatched a plan to creep upon them after dark and scare them. So a mattress went into the canoe and, when it was completely dark, they set out. They were gone over an hour.
>
> I became worried as it was nearly midnight and decided to go after them. But then they returned home. They had Jim's shoes but they were the scared ones for Jim heard them coming and prepared a vociferous welcome. It was not a wonderful success.
>
> August 20: Early this morning I went down to the back harbor to get two rowboats out so I could take one over to George. I was having difficulty as there was a strong north east wind blowing them together. Then, silently round the bend, came Jim and his crew bent on revenge. Taking Nancy by the hand, Jim and the rest silently approached the bunk house. Jim carried in a pail of water and the morning quiet was broken by shouts and shrieks. Jim and his crew hastily took to their canoe, and our three came to an early breakfast after laying out their drenched bedding.
>
> In the afternoon Dick was going over to George's to help caulk

the sailboat. So we all went along, Mike and Steve in the canoe. Betsy and I crossed Mud Channel and picked blueberries on E 19. It had turned out a perfectly beautiful afternoon. One of those late halcyon days, poignant because you would have few like them left for that year. When we returned Mr. Hodgson was there and we all went to the cottage for tea.

We all met on Peace at 7 P.M. ... Dick rowed Betsy and me through the narrow channel, to the inner shore. This course is only possible in high water. When we arrived they were all playing Duck on a Rock, and a bonfire was beginning to blaze. The Groves joined us and soon we were roasting marshmallows and popping corn. Some singing, too. Presently Margaret and David came from a clump of pines, carrying a big paper parcel which they presented to me. It proved to be a lovely Scotch wool pleated skirt (I wore it for years—until the winter of 1971, to be exact). With it was a white birch card signed with all their names and insignia.

It was an evening to be remembered and I said a prayer of thanks to have so many young people around me.

We rowed home outside Peace on a calm sea. The boys were ahead and had the lamps in the cottage lighted for us.

A lovely day—so much appreciated in this summer—so nearly over!

And it was, too. What she does not record is that already, the preceding February, she had ended her long tenure as an island owner by transferring the title to E 3 to her sister, Gwen Erdmann. The last entry in the diary is for August 27 and a few days later Aunt Gladys and Betsy boarded the train for the return trip to St. Louis. She does record the fact that they spent the time in Toronto before the midnight departure of the train to Chicago visiting a horse show—"a good way to pass the time..." The diary concludes with a poem whose source is not given:

I saw the pines

Very beautiful and still and bending over,

Their sharp black heads against a quiet sky.

And there was peace in them.

Bob Donovan and his family were not in residence that summer of 1957 and he writes that he "was busy several years teaching summer sessions to make ends meet." After an interval of four years he and his family returned in 1958.

This was the summer we first had Daisy, and she was a hit all round the bay. Uncle Morris was particularly fond of her, and she was indeed a sweet and good-tempered dog, though she had one uncontrollable vice. She must have been part beagle, because when once she locked onto the scent of a rabbit she became deaf to all command or entreaty. I remember once when she went after a rabbit on E 3 we were unable to call her off, and she disappeared for hours. Eventually we went back to Eagle, and Uncle Morris had to deliver her to us when she finally showed up at their cottage, bedraggled and panting. In those days the butcher at the Ojibway could be prevailed on to throw in a dog bone free with your order, but one of these turned out to be so meaty that Hope made soup out of it and felt guilty afterwards, though whether she thought she had cheated the butcher or the dog remains unclear to me.

I built a makeshift lean-to on the south side of the island, out toward Sunset Point, and Faith and Peter and I decided to sleep out in it one night. Unfortunately Faith got something in her eye and had to retreat to the cottage, but Peter and I stuck it out, and I remember what a man-sized breakfast Peter managed to stow away in the morning. I think we got back to the cottage before anyone else was up. There is something about camping that discourages sleeping late.

The water must have been very low that year, since I remember a swimming expedition to Anderson's beach, which lay mostly out of water. The children enjoyed a chance to play in the warm sand and took turns burying each other up to the neck in sand. Even poor, patient Daisy had to submit to being buried.

It was on the trip home in 1958 that our faithful old Dodge finally gave up the ghost. I think we burned more oil than gasoline on the homeward journey, which incidentally also made us realize how inadequate the car was for our growing family. After supper

7:63. Steve and Maggie French on the deck of their expanded cottage in 1963

we put Faith to bed on the back seat, Peter on the floor (the mound of the drive shaft neutralized with all the dirty laundry), Brian on the ledge of the rear window, and Daisy in the front seat with Hope and me.

The last few years of this period in our history saw the beginning of the expansion of the French cottage on the original Sagastaweekee (fig. 7:63) and the introduction of Sandra, John, and Gary to summers on Georgian Bay (fig. 7:64). Nearby the Wilsons also joined our community. Babs tells the story:

After World War II, in 1945, when he returned to Canada with a wife and son, Allan talked to me many times of this beautiful

7:64. Gary, John, and Sandra French in 1961

part of the country. In 1946 we spent our first vacation at his mother's (then Rhea Flubacher) cottage high on the hill at Pointe au Baril.

From that time on, we spent every vacation at Pointe au Baril. With Flubachers' open Peterborough wooden boat, we were able to make trips to Gronkwa which appealed to us with its isolation and beauty. In 1957 we bought camping equipment which was transported for us by Reids' Marine to the inner side of Hertzberg Island and we had a wonderful holiday with perfect weather. With the Peterborough boat we got to know the whole area well and returned in 1958 and 1959 to camp. In the latter year, having heard that very soon no more Crown land was going to be sold, we decided to go to Parry Sound to get a map showing the islands that were still available for sale. At that time you could only buy an island of more than half an acre and under three acres.

Armed with our map, we cruised the islands and found B 952– 1.6 acres—a good flat area for building and access all around and on the island. A Great Blue Heron was on the shore as we landed for the first time which is why we called the island "Shuh-shuh-gah," Ojibway for blue heron.

We returned to Parry Sound and put a down-payment on B 952 while it was searched and surveyed. Around Christmas time 1959, we received word that the island was ours.

In May of 1960 we had all the lumber delivered by Jerry Evoy's barge and after it was unloaded, it looked as if the whole island was covered with lumber. The area of rock where the cottage was to be built was very flat and needed very little adjustment of the building blocks to make it ready for the timbers and floor of the cottage. With the aid of several friends, but not such cooperation from the weather (it poured with rain most of the weekend!) we were able to get the cottage built. By the time we had to leave, we were able to lock the windows and doors.

That summer was a busy one for us, furnishing the cottage and putting the finishing touches on the inside. Also a dock had to be built to keep our first boat, "Playboy," from dashing up on the rocks (fig. 7:65).

That summer of 1960 was important for me and my family as well. Patricia visited the island for the first time and it was my first trip back in six years. We had an all too brief two weeks. I flew to Detroit from Tallahassee where I had been teaching summer school (Vergil) to be joined by Patricia and baby Kevin (eighteen months) who had been visiting in Cincinnati with her mother. We went on by train to Pointe au Baril where we got off in the dark. We made our way down to Evoy's not realizing that Jerry had gone up to meet us at the station and was snoozing in the waiting room. United at last we headed out to B 980 where we were to share the cottage with Bob and his family. I'll let Bob tell the story, but will offer an explanation for the sleeping arrangement. Kevin was put to bed in a substitute for a crib, the mattress box in the living room with the top removed and one mattress left on the floor. Here Kevin would play as well as sleep, content if enough crackers were handed to him. Here is Bob's version:

The summer of 1960 is memorable for the Gaspe trip in our new red Volkswagen microbus. We set out from Ithaca with no daily

7:65. The famous Wilson boat, "Playboy," with Allan and Babs aboard, 1960s

itinerary planned, and with only two rules guiding our generally northeastward progress: we would stop whenever anyone wanted to, and we would take any and every ferry boat that would lead us in the general direction we wanted to go. Hope and two of the children would sleep in the bus at night, and I (who was too tall to stretch out in the bus) would share a motel (or more often a cabin) with the other child and everyone could use the facilities.

After ten days on the road we arrived, finally, at the Island, where all of us (and particularly Daisy) were anxious to be rid of the car for a while. Unfortunately we arrived in a pelting rain and quickly discovered that it was raining indoors nearly as hard as outdoors. The cottage's ancient roof had given up the unequal struggle with the elements and was leaking copiously. I think we used every pot and pan we had to try to catch the leaks, but the situation was really hopeless. Fortunately the rain stopped next day and we were able to dry out our clothes and bedding.

We lost no time in having a new roof put on, and the men were busy hammering away when Ruth Fisher arrived for a visit on her way to (or from) the Shakespeare festival at Stratford. However, she put up with the din like a good sport, and we enjoyed her stay, though it lasted only a few days.

Bill and Patricia brought little Kevin up that summer, and for some reason Kevin was berthed with me in the living room while his parents slept in the bedroom. Faith, who was eleven, enjoyed having a young cousin to look after.

In 1962, the last year of this period, another newcomer was introduced to the Bay, John H. Watson, the nephew of Peggy Hamilton. Peggy was a year younger than Gladys Dickey and, like her, a school teacher. The original owner of the island, Nokomis, was a school teacher from Toronto, Elizabeth Fuller. Peggy Hamilton was her companion every summer. Over the years my sisters and I always made at least one call at Nokomis each summer with Aunt Gladys. Peggy became the owner in 1937 and one could count on her to have invited a stream of lively guests, most of them fellow teachers, whom we much enjoyed meeting. John Watson provides some names to go with the memories:

> I visited Nokomis for the first time in 1962 at the age of 18 and have been returning annually ever since. Aunt Peggy was introduced to Nokomis by a Miss Fuller. Both were public school teachers in the city of Toronto throughout their working careers. They always spent their entire summers on Nokomis
>
> Aunt Peggy was infamous for her jaunts to the Ojibway, courtesy of her 3.5 HP motor. She was also well known for her many teacher friends, in particular in my recollection, Miss Billingsworth, Betty Hatfield, Edith Hicks, and Miss Jackson. Miss Jackson painted two beautiful pictures of the cottage and they are currently hanging in the main room.

8:66. Bedspring Channel before blasting, April 27, 1963 with Carman Emery

CHAPTER EIGHT

Departures and Arrivals, 1963 - 2000

This period of our story begins, quite literally, with a bang, or I should say, with more than one! That summer of 1963 lightning struck our water pipe and left clear signs of its force in the kitchen. And over behind Carolyn there was an explosive bang as a channel was blasted to permit navigation there. Thanks to the initiative of Steve French, that barrier, as much psychological as real, of the open water was overcome. Gary French recalls that development:

> About this time, Dad was becoming increasingly alarmed that the open water around Carolyn might claim one of us going to or from the Ojibway. The project to blast behind Carolyn in 1963 was in response to this concern (fig. 8:66). It was financed by Dad, Bob Bergs and Dr. Taylor, with great opposition from Dr. Wallace, who resented the traffic behind his island opposite Flatrock at the beginning of Hemlock Channel. Other people contributed on a voluntary basis, including Donovans and

Erdmanns. On a humorous note, I remember swimming through the part in front of Dr. Taylor's where Dad dropped painted milk jugs to mark the channel, when Nancy McDonald came by. Dad wanted to show her how well marked it was and took off, promptly hitting a rock that knocked the propeller off. The total cost was about $2000 —(for the blasting, not repairs to the motor!).

Carrie Bartow also commented in her diary on the opening of this "Bedspring Channel" behind Carolyn that summer and mentions that the Bartows "hit twice going through," so Steve French was not the only one to hit a rock there! Her diary contains references to all the building under way—an A-frame on an island at the southern entrance to Frederic Inlet in 1962, additions to the French cottage that same year, the new boathouse, and, a year or two earlier, the Wilson's cottage. 1963 is a turning point in our history for another reason—that year was the last in which it was possible to purchase crown land. In our area B 979 was the last island bought. While several contributors mention the physical additions during these years, no one likes to remember the human subtractions— islanders who stopped coming or who died in the 1960s. Aunt Gladys made her last visit that cold summer of 1964. Coincidentally that was Leonard Giovannoli's last summer as a regular islander. Carrie wrote in her diary, "Len's last summer up here." 1964 was also the last summer for my father who much enjoyed on his last visit the first of his granddaughter, Maura, not quite one year old. 1965 was the last for Morris and Gwen Erdmann and for Chet Bartow. George Erdmann recalls some of these departures:

When Aunt Gladys got to the age when "she could only do the chores at the Island" she decided that she didn't want to come up any more and she deeded the island to Mother and Dad. They continued to come up for several more years. By this time Dad was retired and they would usually spend the entire summer there. Dad gradually got less and less enjoyment from being in Georgian Bay. He even got to the point that he didn't want to go fishing and that was quite a change for him. He also seemed to suffer the cold more than he did in earlier years. Finally one year as they were leaving he told Mother that that was his last summer; he didn't want to ever come up again. I think that Mother was put out about it as she still loved being there but she couldn't come up alone...

The losses from deaths I recorded earlier, so I will not repeat them, but they made us aware that our human landscape was changing as well as the physical.

The submissions for this history by us older contributors describing our more recent past change as well. Our memories seem to run together and we write summaries of the years, recording the occasional milestone. Bob Donovan comments:

> Oddly enough the summers since 1960 tend to run together in my memory, no doubt because our visits were no longer so widely separated, though I remember missing the summer of 1962, when we moved from Ithaca to Albany, and the summers of 1968 and 1969, at either end of our first year-long sabbatical to Europe. Those summers in the early sixties were chiefly working vacations for Hope and me. I would shut myself up in the bunk house (generally untenanted during those years) and work at The Shaping Vision, which was finally published in 1966, and Hope spent most of her time refinishing boats, while the children were old enough to be turned loose for the day with a lunch and a bathing suit each.

George Erdmann summarizes many years of continuing construction on his island during this period:

> After our basic cottage was up and the porch added, then began a long period of filling in the foundation with stone work. Each summer I would buy at least two bags of cement and then scrounge sand wherever I could find it for the mortar and then make motorboat runs to various islands with small rocks that were available. The water level was critical for both sand and rock collection. Moving the rocks was really work intensive. First they had to be picked up on whatever island or shoal they were available and taken to the boat and loaded. Then I would motor to E 27 and unload them to a shelf that was the right level to make it easier. Then they had to be loaded, just a few rocks at a time in a wheelbarrow, and wheeled to the area where I would

8:67. Mary Ellen
McDonald Baker and
children, 1960s, (l. to
r.), Buff, Wendy (in bow),
Nancy (foreground),
Munch (in arms),
Mary Ellen

be able to use them and then fitted to place. I could usually finish about 10 to 15 feet of foundation each year in the two weeks
that we were there. It was almost a 10 year project with the best
part of 4 years in the fireplace alone. I had a pair of lederhosen
that I had brought back from our first tour in Germany. They
made ideal work pants for the project, being tough enough to
withstand the rock work. After the 10 years, they had had so
much mortar ground into the grain of the leather, they were stiff
as a board!

Sometime during that period the siding of the cottage began to
shrink in the weather. It was a type of shiplap and the shrinkage
opened up cracks between every board. Both rain and mosquitoes had easy access to the living room. Shingles had to be
added to the sides where the porch didn't protect. Then later
more shingles finished the remaining walls.

Also during these early days all of the boats we had either built

8:68. Some of Reid Wilson's "harem" in 1963, (l. to r.), Munch (Martha), Buff, Reid, Wendy

or otherwise accumulated had to be stored in the cottage. Getting them into the living area as we began to ready the cottage for closing was a miserable job. Building a boat house took care of the problem. Carman Emery built a cement and block foundation for me and I erected a very simple structure on a nice sloping rock where boats could be easily pulled up. It was almost a pleasure to close the cottage after that!

In archaeology, the discipline in which I was trained, we estimate the length of a single generation to be about 30 years. In the early to mid 1960s, some 30 years after those first teenagers in our community, another group of youngsters entered that tumultuous time of life. There are some lively descriptions of their social activities. Mary Ellen provides a mother's recollections:

I have left out a great chunk of time when our kids were growing up in Mud Channel and Bake was "commuting" for his two weeks and I was trying desperately to keep up with the kids (fig. 8:67). It is now just one great glorious blur of activity— memorable picnics on Carolyn, the sand bar in Frederic Inlet, and the lovely beach on Shawanaga Bay, the endless nights lying awake or knitting while I awaited that lovely sound of the canoe bumping against the dock and the muted voices as my teenagers stumbled up the dark path. There are endless stories!

A father, Bob Donovan, recalls the particular social activity of one summer, that of 1963:

The summer of 1963 was the year of Reid Wilson's "harem" (fig. 8:68). He bombed around the bay in the Playboy, accompanied, usually, by a bevy of girls which included Faith, Wendy and Buff Baker, Gwen Erdmann, and occasionally Molly Erdmann, though I think Molly tended to regard the other girls as too young and frivolous to be associated with. One night the girls had a slumber party in the bunk house, and on another occasion they camped out at the end of Fayola. Hope was concerned about Reid's nocturnal visitation of the camp site, but she needn't have worried. After dark that evening we heard a voice call over the water, "It's all right, Mrs. Donovan, I'm going home now."

In Carrie Bartow's diary one finds the word, "hootenanny," appearing for the first time in 1965 (Faith Donovan and Gwen Erdmann had arrived by canoe to invite Carrie to one at the Erdmanns'). And in 1967 she speaks of a birthday party at her brother's (Harry Zahn's) cottage on Little Winona at which Reid played his guitar, while his father Allan played the harmonica. One of the young people, Gary French, remembers some of the fun:

My sister Sandra (b. 1951) and brother John (b. 1952) and I had many friends growing up at the island. Dad's penchant for relaxation through work, (building), precluded us from being away a great deal, but I certainly recall my closest contemporaries as David Erdmann, Brian Donovan and, later, Steve Malone. My father, with affection, always referred to Brian Donovan as "Little Einstein."

My sister was friends with David Erdmann's sister Gwen, so the traffic back and forth was by sail and canoe to Sagastaweekee, and by power from Sagastaweekee, until David's father George equipped one of their beautifully "George-made" prams with one of the slowest, noisiest motors ever invented. Our family usually figured that we needed to begin breakfast within 5 minutes of hearing David's motor in order to have the table cleared by his arrival time at Sagastaweekee. Our legacy to the area is a tree fort on E 27, not of the calibre Pete McDonald built in his childhood.

Brian Donovan and I became friends early on. In an effort to improve communications between Frenches and Donovans, a genuine "cottage industry" emerged. Brian arrived one summer with a red, plastic water and air propelled rocket. My mother was terrified that it might well make it across French's Bay, but I never recall it making it much closer than 50 yards off the "diving" rock, on which B 937 is painted.

On the other hand, Sandra and Brian's older brother, Peter, had developed a simple, fool-proof system to communicate—towels—a red one meant stay away and a white one meant come over. They were a "summer friendship" and surveillance was apparently undertaken by the respective mothers.

I remember choking with laughter at breakfast one morning upon learning that Sandra and Peter had planned to go "star watching" one night at midnight, only to be intercepted by the person at the other end of the cigarette glow in the night, my mother! The question put to the night air was, "and just where do you think you're going?"

Brian Donovan and I planned a camping trip one year but found ourselves in a terrible wind and rain storm. So we sailed down Mud Channel and crawled under our overturned canoe on Riley's Rock and popped some popcorn. It seemed strange that there were so many boats out but it never occurred to us that my family, Brian's and George Erdmann would be looking for us. We were not terribly popular when we surfaced!

Of course adults also mark some milestones over these years, often associated with a new boat, a major addition to the cottage, or the like. Bob Donovan writes:

The summer of 1964 was made memorable by the acquisition

8:69. Andy and Marcie McDonald with their fox snake, "Poppa," 1960s

of the Eaglet (a sailing dinghy), now, alas, defunct, but then resplendent in its white and blue paint.

In the summer of 1965 the water was extraordinarily low—so low that the sand bottom of the channel by Anderson's was out of water, creating a huge sandbank, where we had some memorable swimming parties. I remember the children burying each other in the sand, and Pete McDonald exhibiting his athletic prowess by balancing Marcie on his hands.

During those summers when Patricia and I were so frequently in Greece, Pete and Nancy once or twice used the Baker cottage on Wabassin. Then, for several years Pete and his family were up every summer, as he recalls:

The summers of 1966 through 1969, Bob Bergs offered his cot-

8:70. George Erdmann at the helm of Gryphon, late 1960s

tage to me and my first wife, Nancy, when she was very ill. I remember that Marcie (b. 1958) and Andy (b. 1960) would sit out on the big rock in the evening and sing across the water to the Baker girls who would then sing back.

I also remember that Bob had a large aquarium in which Andy kept a huge fox snake named Poppa (fig. 8:69). Early one morning Andy came in all excited, calling, "Poppa's a Momma." She had laid lots of eggs.

One set of milestones in the history of our community has been provided by a series of sailboats belonging to George Erdmann. Indeed it is impossible to think of him at the island without also thinking of his love of sailing. After the snipe came the Gryphon (fig. 8:70), then the Water Rat, and last of all Saucy ("she always likes to show her bottom!"). Bob Donovan comments on the importance of the Gryphon to our communal life:

George brought the Gryphon up in the summer of 1966, and we all enjoyed sailing in it. It made the trip to the McCoys or even to the Limestones an easy–though not less exciting—excursion.

George himself contributes an account of the beginning and of the end of this beloved vessel:

I have fond memories of the sailboat Gryphon. While we were still stationed in Hawaii I found a picture in a book about small boats. It had been designed by a New Englander but when I wrote to him to buy plans he had died without ever making detailed drawings. I did like the looks of the boat so much that I spent hours taking measurements from the tiny picture in the book and making lines, plans and profiles. When we returned to Denver for the next tour, I expanded the plans to full size lofting plans and began to build the hull. It was built on a platform in the backyard of our house. It was finished by the second year of our Denver tour and ready to tow up to the Island. I set out a mooring right off of the front of E 27 and it was always a pleasure to be able to look out of the cottage and see it floating there. It was a very easy boat to sail. All of the sails were self-tending in that the boat could tack from port to starboard tack without my ever having to handle any of the sheets. It was easy to tack out of almost any channel against the wind while sailing alone. The little one lung engine that I installed was not the most powerful, only giving about five and a half or six miles per hour. It made for a long trip in to the Station when we wanted to go — almost two hours. Even though it was only twenty feet long it would hold a gang of people. Several times we would sail out to the Limestones with eight or nine people aboard. It was a little low in the water and somewhat sluggish but it managed.

After I had built the Water Rat and had it at the Island, I decided that doing maintenance on two fairly large boats was just too much and I decided to sell the Gryphon. Allan Wilson heard about the sale and bought it for Reid and Peter. I still had the trailer that I had used to tow the Gryphon; in fact I used it to haul the boat into the boat house for winter storage. They got several inner tubes and fastened them under the frame of the trailer and floated it back to the Station behind a boat. Peter used the Gryphon for several years and then one winter he had a fire in his garage and the masts were destroyed. When he got bids for replacements the cost was astronomical, so he sold the hull for what he could get for it. So ended the Gryphon.

Newly settled in Minnesota by 1967 and, having a summer off from our work in Greece, Patricia and I with Kevin and Maura finally arranged another visit. For the first time we had the island to ourselves. My sisters, Didge and Betsy, were over on the Erdmann island, E 3, and Bob and his family arrived to occupy Eagle after we had left. Kevin writes about his memories of our trips from Minnesota to Pointe au Baril and especially that first one in 1967:

These are some of the memories I have over the past 30 years. I am third generation Island. I have been told the stories of times past when it was truly an adventure just to get to the Island we call Eagle. It seems that over time Island memories blend together and things that happened two years ago could have, in fact, happened ten years ago.

Some of my most vivid memories involve the feelings leading up to a trip to the Island. The feeling got most acute after the last snow had melted and the trees were beginning to show signs of new life. Sitting in class daydreaming of catching frogs in Didge's swamp. Thoughts of casting out that new Daredevil spoon to a hungry pike. All pushed out any notion of learning about the Sioux Indian Wars. Two weeks before we left it would be time to assemble all the things needed for the Island. Two flashlights for sure, five or six red and white spoons (mighty pikes eat up great numbers of fishing lures and so do rocks and weeds). The minor things such as clothes Papa would always pack. Adults seemed to have a different outlook to trip preparation. Mother and Papa would never, seemingly, do anything until the last moment. Then on the last night they would stay up all night sorting and resorting food and supplies. Mother would make sandwiches to pacify the passengers in the back seat.

Finally the big day would come. Good-bye St. Paul—hello the Island! One year's departure I particularly remember is 1967. (We Donovans are usually ten years behind; we were driving a 57 Chevy.) That year we planned to leave on the Fourth of July, or so we thought. We awoke early to finish our loading of the car.

Maura and I would carry bags down to the car where Papa would pack them into the trunk like pieces of a very difficult jigsaw puzzle. After loading the car we walked around the house making sure everything was OK for the summer. I always hoped the neighborhood kids would see us leaving. Most of them never left the confines of ding dong ditch over the long hot summer nights in St. Paul. Well, on this particular grand departure day our leaving was not to happen. Some very low-down dirty motorhead had stolen our 57 Chevy's distributor cap. I wasn't sure exactly what this part did for the car, but I did know it messed up our leaving for the Island. We had a Fiat which was in no way able to carry a family of four plus supplies 800 miles to the Island. Papa and I went out to look for a distributor cap but, alas, because it was a holiday we did not have any luck.

Finally we would be on the road. As soon as we would turn the corner from our street onto Lexington Avenue, the sandwiches would begin to flow to the back seat and hungry mouths. The drive to the Island was exactly 810 miles. I think my love for geography comes in part from these road trips. Once across the St. Croix River there was no turning back; we really were on the way to the Island! At the first gas stop we would all pile out to use the facilities except for Mother who would never darken the door of a filling station washroom. The other big excitement at gas stops for Maura and me was to get maps which were free. So, of course, we got one of each times two. These maps, plus the never-ending sandwiches, kept us occupied for most of the trip.

The towns, incorporated and unincorporated, all across Wisconsin are ingrained in my memories of driving Highway 8. Cameron (right turn), Baron (turkey capital of the world), Catawba (not to be confused with the grape of the same name) are all towns on this route. Papa would always stop for gas when the gauge read half empty. Thus, Maura and I had ample opportunity to increase our map collections. I do not to this day understand why a gas station in Rhinelander, Wisconsin, needed to stock road maps of Louisiana, but Maura and I were beneficiaries of this foresight.

As we continued across Wisconsin we passed through Laona (on the Rat River). Towards evening we crossed into U.P. Michigan at the town of Norway near an iron mine. After dinner in a McDonald's we would be ready for the "find the motel saga." Manistique has the distinction of being half way to the Island. The town is on the northwest coast of Lake Michigan. As a consequence of this location there are many motels to choose from. We must have seen them all. The criteria for the targeted motels were rigid: the beds must be firm and the decor had to be vintage 50s. Maybe, if we were really lucky, we would have the "magic fingers" option on the bed. The other neat thing would be color TV; at home we sported a Zenith 12 inch black and white. The bottom line, however, would always be the price.

The next morning we would wake early with dew still on the windshield and drive on towards the island. Papa liked to leave at the crack of dawn, while the rest of us were still mostly asleep. Slowly the landscape changed as we drove farther east. The excitement and anticipation would grow with every passing mile post. Tonight we would be brushing our teeth over the juniper bushes!

The next big moment was the crossing into Canada at the Sault. A note here about rest stops: the Michigan Tourist Board has built one of the finest bathrooms ever at the border crossing. On Mother's and Maura's scale it rates five stars, an honor not given lightly! Sault Saint Marie is two cities, one in Michigan, the other in Ontario, separated by a toll bridge that passes over the locks and the rapids of the St. Mary's River that connects Lakes Superior and Huron. After crossing the bridge we would have to check through Canadian customs, always a nervous experience. The border guards always asked if we had anything to declare. Papa would wear coat and tie (a hold over from the "old days" when people had to dress up to travel) and the rest of us would sit erectly in our seats pretending to be very nonchalant about the whole affair.

The "we are in Canada now" feeling just heightened the excitement of getting to the Island. The route follows the North Channel (the upper part of Georgian Bay). We would pass through the towns of Bruce Mines, Spanish, and Espanola. Maura and I played road games in the back seat; a favorite was looking for signs with the letters A through Z in sequential order. The next clue that the island was getting closer was the smokestacks of Sudbury. These monsters of industry produced clouds of smoke signaling the smelting of ore to extract nickel. With the exception of the supermarkets and highrises, the scenery of the town of Sudbury was very much how I would envision the lunar landscape.

Now would come the most stressful part of the whole trip: the marketing for the first three weeks at the Island. I always had very strong beliefs about what the culinary menu should include. I wanted that good hearty food like baloney and "Wonder Bread," not peanut butter and jelly on whole grain.

After shopping at two stores to get the best buys we would be ready for the final push to the Island. The distance we had left to drive was less than 80 miles, but this last stretch seemed longer than the odometer ever showed. The highway curves and winds through the rock of the Canadian Shield. There are few signs of the beauty that lies just a little farther ahead. French River, Britt, we are so close. All eyes are straining to see that last turn and the view down the hill that means we have arrived at the Pointe.

Bob Donovan and his family followed us that summer as occupants of the old cottage on Eagle. He recalls some of the highlights of their stay:

In some ways the most hilarious time of all was the summer of 1967, when Didge made her famous movie on Carolyn. I'm sure others will write about that memorable occasion, so I won't enlarge on it, though I have vivid memories of Brian riding a bicycle off the edge of the island into the water, and Peter, managing to capsize the Eaglet in a flat calm. That was the summer, too, when we hosted a regatta, for which Brian created beautiful blue and red and gold prize ribbons and a blank "Grand Prize Certificate" which we still have.

Our records skip a year (we were in Greece that entire summer), but Carrie Bartow comments the following year, 1969, on the price of propane ($15 for 100 lbs.), a new picnic area on the Shawanaga side of Big Island, and the sale of "Reid's old island" (B

8:71. The Curry Family in their cottage, 1980, (l. to r.), Fran, Eric, Melissa, Dudley

921). Her comment was that the owner, Leland Morton, was "asking $15,000. Wow!" (her favorite exclamation). The new owners were Fran and Dudley Curry (fig. 8:71); the latter describes the transfer:

> Island B 921 was known locally as "the Haunted House," or the "Eagle's Nest," as far as we have heard. Since we've never seen a haunt or an eagle's nest on the island, we decided to name it "Little Camp" (Petitkuwa) because it sits on the "Gronkwa" (Great Camp) which is also called Frederic Inlet. According to our word of mouth sources Gronkwa was the site of the annual fur traders rendezvous, furnishing protection from storms from every direction.

> Fran and I came to own Petitkuwa because of Harry Zahn, now deceased, of Island B 856, purchased next by Graham and Maja Willoughby of Winnipeg. In 1969 Fran and I were guests on the island E 5 owned by Jean and David Hofmann. We set out in a canoe one day to try to find an island of our own. We paddled through Tug Channel and Harry Zahn waved to us from his kitchen window. Yelling back and forth, we asked him if he knew of an island that might be for sale. He said that his brother-in-law who lived in Orlando, Florida, wanted to sell B 921, and he gave us Mr. Morton's phone number. We paddled to the Ojibway phone booth that afternoon, called Mr. Morton who gave us a very low asking price, and we bought the island on the phone.

8:72. Allan Wilson acquired his red and white Cessna airplane in 1971

Lawyers settled the deal by mail. We had the old haunted house torn down and a new cottage built in 1970 by Carman Emery. So we are the third owners since the original owner Olver Reid (actually held in the name of Olver Reid's father, J. M. Reid) sold the island to Mr. Morton (in 1960).

In 1971 Carrie Bartow noted that the Wilsons had sold their "big boat" and acquired a "red and white Cessna" airplane capable of "95 MPH." (fig. 8:72) She also mentioned that Gary French was employed that summer at Wings, while brother John worked for Wallace Reid. Gary recalls those summer jobs:

My brother John and I spent many summers working up North, John at Reid's Marine, while I toiled at Desmasdons and Wings.

This gave us the opportunity to become fast friends with many year-round residents as well as the urge to explore beyond our area. I attribute this time to my annual trips around the Bay— north to Killarney, Little Current, the North Channel and the Soo and south to Parry Sound, Honey Harbour and up the Bruce Peninsula to Lion's Head and Tobermory.

My trips around Pointe au Baril at night with Wallace Reid, to learn more about mechanical things, to Osawa Island and the

8:73. Conclusion of the Treasure Hunt, 1971. (l.to r.), Bob Donovan, Mary Ellen and Nancy Baker, George Erdmann (Ollie) "beheading" Allan Wilson (Chuck), Faith and Brian Donovan

Twin Sisters were fun. Spending the night at Reid's home at the Station meant learning to appreciate the blending of precision thinking and mechanical aptitude. It lets one appreciate Wally Reid's handmade radio sets and radio-controlled sailboats. Wally and Bruce Reid are two great local personalities.

Over the years cottagers of all ages have gathered to take part in a favorite game. Fortunately Bob Donovan provides a written record of one these memorable games—the Treasure Hunt of 1971:

On Friday, July 30, 1971, at Eagle Island, a treasure hunt was conducted, pitting the Cavaliers, captained by Allan Wilson (Chuck), against the Roundheads, captained by George Erdmann (Ollie). After a breathless chase of over three miles, lasting nearly an hour, the Roundheads discovered the treasure (a loaf of cinnamon bread, baked by Hope Donovan), and upon the return of the opposing team, Chuck was duly beheaded (fig. 8:73).

The Cavaliers: Allan Wilson, Captain, Mary Ellen Baker, Faith

Donovan, Peter Donovan, David Erdmann, Molly Erdmann, Richie Nord.

The Roundheads: George Erdmann, Captain, Nancy Baker, Timmy Baker, Brian Donovan, Hope Donovan, Reid Wilson.

The Clues

Cavaliers	Roundheads
Old Riley lived a life of ease,	To rid oneself of trash these days,
A thing that's hard to knock,	In ways both safe and legal,
But what surprises me is this:	Is there no remedy beside
His name's linked with a rock.	Relying on the seagull?
At cradles rocking in the waves	The walls of Troy rose to the sound
No purist needs to jib,	Of music by Apollo,
But what are we to make of this:	An act that Clinton Grove once found
A stationary crib?	Was difficult to follow.
Lord Minton was an English peer,	Lord Minton was an English peer,
Whose 'scutcheon bore no blot;	Whose 'scutcheon bore no blot;
However good Lord Minton he	However good Lord Minton he
Emphatically was not.	Emphatically was not.
The board was placed upon the stones,	Like grounded gull or rockbound seal,
The stones upon the brink;	Or whale upon the strand,
From board one leaped into the air,	The silver fish beside the house
Then plunged into the drink.	Is impotent to land.
Though eagles proudly mount the sky,	Though eagles proudly mount the sky,
As poets long have sung,	As poets long have sung,
At close of day they sink back down	At close of day they sink back down
To tend their fledgling young.	To tend their fledgling young.

Since many of these clues refer to places or things that are no longer in existence, it may be appropriate to add a few explanatory notes. Riley's Rock scarcely requires a note, but the old dump site on island 500 A that nearly everyone used, probably does. The crib in the next clue was the log crib Steve French set up in French's Bay to mark a shoal that Maggie had hit once too often at night. Clinton Grove's wall is, I think, still self-explana-

8:74. Eric Curry and
Nancy Baker in 1972.

tory, and everyone knows the Badminton Court on Eagle Island, behind the bunk house. The stone platform on Chinook once held a diving board, though not everyone will remember this. The "silver fish" is perhaps the most ephemeral clue of all; it referred to Uncle Morris's aluminum boat, which spent the entire summer upside down beside the cottage on E 3. The Eaglet was beached conspicuously near the back dock on Eagle, and I prudently waited until the hunt had started before putting the carefully wrapped cinnamon loaf inside. Lest anyone think I shirked the chase, I laid both trails by canoe in the very first light of dawn.

In her diary for that same summer Carrie noted that John and Denise Watson were visiting his aunt, Peggy Hamilton, on Nokomis. The entry for the following summer, 1972, indicates that the Currys were in residence on Petitkuwa with their son "Eric, about 17; he has long curley hair, Wow! (fig. 8:74)" The water must have been high that year for she wrote that the Currys had paddled through the "back channel" (between 500 A and Big Island) to the Ojibway. 1974 was made memorable by a visit, his first in ten years, from Leonard Giovannoli. He camped for about three weeks in late July and early August near the picnic area on Big Island facing Shawanaga. The records list many social gatherings and many children during the 1970s The following summary by Bob Donovan brings us to the end of the decade:

> The summer of 1972 was a tough one for Brian, who had to wear a back brace all summer because of a compression fracture of the fifth and sixth vertebrae, the result of a bicycle accident. Fortunately, he was able to remove the brace for swimming. This was the summer we introduced Jenny and Alice to the Island. Both of them took to the life at once, even Alice, who proved a formidable mouser, and who enjoyed reeling and writhing on the bare rock in the moonlight. They did complicate our lives on the trip, however, since we took two days each way, instead of the one long day we usually managed to do it in. On the way up Hope realized that she had forgotten her glasses when we were at Herkimer, seventy-five miles from Albany, so there was nothing to do but go back, which of course meant stopping overnight near Parry Sound. Motels are not particularly restful if you have to tend to the needs of a puppy and a kitten. The night before we were scheduled to leave the Island a storm came up, and it blustered and rained all night. We had a terrible time locating Alice when Jerry's boat was due to arrive, but we managed to get away reasonably on time, only to find at the Station that the road a couple of miles south of Pointe au Baril had washed out in the storm and was impassable. At that time no alternative route was practicable, so we had to wait by the side of the road while a long procession of trucks brought gravel to dump in the flooded roadway. By the time we were able to proceed it was so late that we could get no farther than Toronto, but fortunately the Wilsons were home and offered us their warm and generous hospitality.
>
> I'll pass over several years, noting only that we missed the summer of '75, when we went to England for the year, but we brought Betsy Donovan and her son Jan back with us, and they both came up to the Island in '76. The next year was made

memorable for everyone in the bay by the arrival of the Water Rat, and our photo album is full of shots of the wonderful cruise we all took. We missed the summer of '78 because of our long western tour that year, but we came back in '79 to find Bill and family at home in their new cottage, the Theke.

Before I leave the 1970s, however, there are several other important events to record. Carrie Bartow noted in her diary the comings and goings in our community for the last time in 1976. After that summer she did not return to her beloved island. In 1977 Gary French, now the new owner of the old Giovannoli island (B 945), began the first of a series of improvements to the old cottage. Then, in the summer of 1979, two of our islanders began a romance that led to marriage. To begin with Gary's account:

> Our family had never done anything with Kenusa, save building a sun deck and dock when it was purchased in 1964. So, by the time I bought it in 1977, it was in a terrible state of disrepair— no roof shingles, rotting walls and full of junk (that our family stored there) with some of the original treasures that the Giovannolis left when it was sold to Dad (including a rattlesnake's head and rattles in a bottle).

> The original building dates to 1914 and there appears to have been about seven additions, no mean feat in a building of just a few hundred square feet. It has proved a challenge to try to retain its charm and character while modernizing it to the point of comfort for the amount of time we spend there.

> It is my goal to be at the island each year within 48 hours of the departure of the ice and to return when the ice is solid enough. I have been at it in every single month of the year, a claim very few people can make, or even want to make. It is the fact that I am there so often that made it important that the cottage be made heatable in winter for which it was never intended and that it should have a few comforts and conveniences for summer use as well.

> My love of boats, all boats, is obvious by their numbers but few people know that I take great pride in the boats our family has introduced to Pointe au Baril, including the Boston Whaler, the

Thornes aluminium boat, the KMV, the Mederios, and the Musling. With my trips and enjoyment of rough seas, these boats have all appealed to my sense of adventure and survival instincts. I would be remiss if I didn't dispel the notion of the Frenches as only "powerboat" people. My grandfather was a member of the War Canoe Champions of Canada team in 1913 for the Parkdale Canoe Club, and evidence of this hangs in the sleeping cabin I built some years ago. I enjoy spring and fall canoeing more than in the summer because the bugs bother me less then.

Wendy Malone Hofmann contributes her account of the romance linking her family to that of the Hofmanns:

Time went by and Helen Grove's daughter Nancy had six kids, one of whom was I, Wendy, and Dickie's Jeannie (really Ralph and Dorothy Foutz's Jeannie!) had five kids, one of whom was Steve. Although I spent many parts of summers on the island with either my family or my grandmother, Steve and his family usually came up later in the summer, and our paths never crossed until the summer of 1979. I will never forget the day I met Steve for the first time. I had come out to Fayola's dock on Evoy's boat with my Aunt Judy and various family members during a three-day blow. Going around Turning Rock, the waves were crashing over the top of Evoy's taxi! Just a tad frightening. After we were safely deposited on Fayola, a contingent of Hofmanns boated on up to greet us. "Where's Steve?" someone asked. "Oh, he's swimming up," someone else replied. Yes, swimming up, right in the middle of a very blowy storm. Well, Steve swam up to the dock, hauled his Arnold Schwartzenegger body out of the water, and gave me a most shy look. "This guy," I thought, "is crazy." That opinion has not changed.

Well, about two years later Steve and I were married at Ralph and Dorothy's home in Tiffin, Ohio, with many family members exclaiming over the turn of events that made our getting together possible. We would not be so happily married to each other if it were not for Paul Pope who knew Ethel Williams who knew Helen Lewandowski Grove who knew Dickie Foutz who is the aunt of Jeannie Foutz Hofmann who is the mom of Steve, and of course, back to Helen who is the mom of my mom, Nancy.

I'm sure glad it all happened. Now, B 985 is related by blood to B 987 (Fayola), E 18 (Chinook), and E 5 (Kingbird), and related by spirit to B 1000 (Wabassin) and B 937 (Timbers/Wabanonge), for if it were not for Ethel Williams, aunt of Pete McDonald and Ben Baker, none of the Groves, Kochs, Malones, Hofmanns, Franklins, or Currys would be part of the idyllic village that is our little corner of Georgian Bay.

The years after 1980 produced events, both joyous and sad, pointing to changes still to come. First, one notes the changes in island ownership. During this period several islands previously owned by others passed into different hands. In 1982 the former French island, B 937, was sold to the Bakers and McDonalds. This purchase marked the beginning of a new chapter both for the island and for Pete as he recounts:

> For me my ties to this area and to family and friends here fall into three distinct periods of my life. First, there were the growing-up years on Aunt Ethel's (Williams) island, Chinook. During the next period, I stayed at the Baker's Wabassin cottage with my then young children, Marcie and Andy, and wife Nancy. Bob Bergs also shared his cottage with us for a couple of summers. Following Nancy's death, the visits and memories were interrupted.

> Then I met Linda, and after a "shake-down" trip to the islands, it became clear that this area would be an important part of our life together. We were married, and there were six of us. Linda and I decided to take the plunge and purchase an island, or at least half of an island. We bought the French's island of Sagastaweekee from the then owner, Paul Phelan (the island was listed under the name of Phelan's daughter, Rosemary Anne Phelan). Son Todd renamed the island Timbers because of its unusual number of trees. This purchase marked the creation of a new island history for me with Linda that includes new family, personal memories, and additional wonderful friends.

> Linda's sons, Todd and Brad, had camping experiences at Camp Adanac on Manitoulin Island, so we were off and running, or at

least paddling! Now, Linda who first felt like a newcomer to the Bay, is showing me a new dimension to our love for the area and for each other. It's awfully easy to take each for granted, but this place provides a good opportunity to reflect on how well off we are in so many ways.

Since we purchased the island soon after our marriage, we had two households of furniture, so Timbers got the leftovers. Andy drove a U-Haul up to the Pointe with cottage furnishings, and we started our island life with the addition of new roofs, floors and kitchen. Stone steps from the dock to the cottage were a priority that Brad and Andy crafted with a little help from Dad. We all worked on major paths around the island including Linda's Lane and Andy's Autobahn. Linda began to identify most of the plants on the island and pressed them just as my brother Dix did years ago. Her identification process was aided with patient assistance from Bill and Patricia Donovan, Fran and Dudley Curry, and countless books with pictures of blooming plants!

Brad's sailing experience from Adanac led us into sailing an Albacore bought from Frank and Layne Hardy. Our skills were limited, and we sold the boat to Kevin Donovan; it was more than we could handle! A Hobie-cat is now more our style. In addition, we have a loan from Carol and Bill Prior, a beautiful Cosine Weary cedar rowboat, great for exercise and morning fishing.

Summers at the island (as we bring our story up to the present) are marked with visits from Andy from Florida, and Brad and wife Sharon from Cleveland. Brad has introduced Sharon to island life. Time has added a "new" screened porch and decks, solar power for a phone and running water, and a succession of composting toilets. All make life easier, thanks to Linda, in spite of my feelings that Ethel got along just fine without all of those niceties. The airtight insert in the fireplace has made our annual Thanksgiving visit and dinner at the Frenches' much more comfortable.

We look forward to the sharing of stories from our friends in this history. We have a very special area where we are able to share generations of friends, memories, and the place itself.

Brownie Baker contributes her own account of the purchase

of Sagastaweekee and of her ties to this island that began so many years before when she began to explore on her own in the famous little red canoe.

> In those early years I ventured out of Mud Channel and found wonderful exploring places, my favorite being the highest rock on French's Island, Sagastaweekee (the French family not being in residence for many years). What delicious memories I have of reading, dreaming and enjoying the spectacular view from my special spot. How ironic that my special dreaming place is situated on what is now our half of Sagastaweekee which Pete, Linda, Bake, and I bought in 1982. In 1985 we built Wabanonge Cottage ("place of the sunrise") on the northeast corner of the island. This cottage has been a godsend when any of our five children, with their families, visit. How great to be able to be together, but not together all the time!

A similar transfer occurred in 1986 when the Currys acquired the Bartow island (B 919). Increasingly common are changes in ownership when a title is passed to other members of the immediate or extended family. Allan and Babs Wilson in 1980 transferred the title of their island to Reid and Margaret. The change in ownership of the old Dickey/Erdmann island (E 3) illustrates the old complication (Dickey/Whitelaw) of shared property, a complication more of us are facing. As families grow and young people mature, and with no crown land available for purchase, suddenly extended families are confronting a challenge. George Erdmann's story provides one example:

> Mother transferred title to E 3 to Jim and me (in 1959) and it stayed in our names for a few years (until 1969). Joint ownership always seems to create problems, especially when only one of the owners is really active in coming up. Jim was living in Denver and had a summer cabin in Pike National Forest and had converted to being a mountain man. He had no objection to ownership but the costs of maintaining a cottage which he no longer used became increasingly burdensome. Finally when Sue and I were in Germany for the last time, from 1968 to 1971, Jean Erdmann contacted me by letter to ask if I still wanted to buy

them out. I had offered to do so many times before. I did and had the title transferred to my name only in 1969.

Molly, David, and Gwen were coming up when they could and they could use the cottage on E 3. We all finally decided that we would transfer title to them and let them take on the burden of maintaining the cottage. Again multi-ownership proved to be a problem. Other interests and constraints on the time and money of the three new owners led to unequal usage and the burdens of record keeping and billing fell to one, Molly. She was stuck with the work of taking care of all the details.

After long consideration we decided that if we expanded the capacity of E 27 so that Molly, Gwen, and David could have space there when they did want to come up then we could sell E 3. Steve and Sarah Donovan had been looking for an island for some years, so Molly offered them the option (1986). They jumped at the chance and title was again transferred. I built a small bunk house in the same position that the old Read cottage had occupied. It sleeps 4 people and, with a tent covering on one end, they had a small bug-proof area to relax in.

In this instance the problems of joint ownership were too difficult, but the final transfer was typically within the family (between cousins). Steve and Sarah, by the purchase of E 3, escaped some of the problems of joint ownership over on the Donovan island, B 980, where I and my four siblings together with our spouses and children have been finding ways to coexist. Scheduling, seeking agreement on maintenance, record keeping and billing, all were new tasks and all can lead to disagreements. There are, however, the compensating advantages of shared costs and more frequent contacts between family members otherwise widely dispersed across the continent.

Steve and Sarah escaped the difficulties of shared ownership when they acquired E 3, but they were quickly introduced to two of the hazards feared by all cottagers, fire and lightning, as Sarah tells us:

Our story begins on a dark and stormy night—well, not exactly. It was actually shortly after dinner with Steve's parents and brother's family on B 980. As my mother-in-law and I stood in the kitchen finishing dishes, there was an unexpected bolt of lightning that split the view from the window and an instant clap of thunder. We made the usual observation, "Wow, that was close!" and thought nothing more of it other than being relieved that there was no rain to paddle back home in. We stayed another hour or so and then innocently set off for E 3.

As we approached our cottage through the deepening dusk, we noticed something was awry. We peered more intently and saw to our surprise that the south window shutters were loose and not completely attached to the cottage anymore. Again suspecting nothing (now past innocence and into stupidity), we were amazed that the "wind" had been so strong here when it hadn't been that much at Eagle. Entering the cottage, we found that a lone glass had fallen from the dish shelves and broken, and then that those bad banging shutters had broken the 2 windows in Katie's room. Well! Who would have thought!

A family member who shall remain unnamed insists that we realized shortly thereafter that the lightning had struck our cottage. However, since I am the one chronicling this event, we shall go with the official version (mine), which is that it wasn't until the next morning in the daylight when we figured it out. You could see the path the lightning took. The old pine midway along the screened porch on the east side had a gash with singed edges that was several feet long. The lightning had traveled part way down the tree, jumped to the edge of the roof, traveled around to the south side, and exited through the floor of Julie's room. We also later saw burn marks traveling along the rock to some old cable wire left over from a long ago dock. As we looked that morning at the damage, it was frightening. The windows in Katie's room hadn't broken. They had exploded. There were not only the shards of glass on her pillow that we had seen the night before, but small slivers were embedded in the wall of her room across from the windows. In Julie's room, the lightning had gone through the foot of her bed. The blanket, sheets, and mattress top each had a jagged hole, again with burn marks. The floor of her room had a chunk blown out of it. And though we looked and looked, not believing our eyes, there was no exit hole in the mattress. Frank Penfold told us later the the entire cottage had moved a sixteenth of an inch; you could see where the supports

8:75. The McConnell Family, summer, 1994, (l. to r.), Nancy, Tom, Lisa, Shirley

had shifted, exposing previously covered rock.

Did I mention yet that this was 1987, our very first summer in our own cottage?

This was on a Tuesday. Friday afternoon we were once again at Eagle, having gone over for a swim. As we relaxed on the porch, Brownie and her little green motorboat appeared and she waved frantically at us. We heard her shout, "There's a fire on E 3" and she was gone! As the McDonalds later described to us, when they saw all thirteen of the Donovan clan swarm out of the cottage and take off at a run for the back dock, it looked as if someone had stepped on an anthill. By the time we got to our cottage, there were several people with buckets already there and the fire was no longer blazing. Forgive me for not remembering all of you. I have a clear vision of George Erdmann pumping a fire hose, and the rest is a blur. Everyone hauled buckets of water for quite a time, trying to ensure that the fire was truly out. Someone relieved George at the pump. I had caught a large catfish the day before that was residing in the fish cage. Since the end of the water hose kept floating up, someone had used the cage as a weight to keep it submerged, never noticing the poor fish inside. I mainly remember how EVERYONE came to help. I don't believe that before that day I had realized that our French's Bay area is a small, close-knit community. Our lives have become intertwined forever through our summers on the bay. It is a closeness that I treasure. We are all family.

In 1990 the last "new" family to join our community (up to time of writing) arrived. The McConnells, however, were not new to the region, only to our part of it (fig. 8:75). That year they purchased and built on the island we always called "The Dairy Queen" or the "Hot Dog Stand" (B 979). Tom summarizes their history:

> 1975 to 1982, purchased a cottage from Alan Wainwright in Sturgeon Bay (Duck Bay), S 121 on older maps. Sold cottage in 1984 to Mr. Gunn.
>
> 1981 to 1991, purchased lot on Laura Bay north of the Lighthouse from Cooper. Built one cottage in 1982, a second in 1983 (builder, Stan Demasdon), currently renting.
>
> 1990 to the present, purchased Island B 979, "The Hot Dog Stand," from Karen Hodgson (nee Tiffin). Removed old cottage, fall, 1990, that had been built by her father in 1963. Built 2 sleeping cottages and 1 main cottage in 1991. Added tent platform with walls, July, 1992. Moved in, May, 1992.
>
> Why are we here? We originally stayed with friends at Key Harbour and stopped in Pointe au Baril on our way home and purchased our first cottage. We then became very active at the Ojibway Club—Shirley put together as a fund raiser the Cottage Cook Book; Tom served for 6 years on the Board of the Club and was President in 1987; Lisa and Nancy attended programs starting at age 6 and went on later to work at the Club.

In these last decades there have been departures as well as arrivals. Carrie Bartow's last summer followed by that of her son and heir, Chet, Jr., has already been mentioned. In 1982 there was another loss. Babs Wilson writes:

In the summer of 1983, after Allan's death in October 1982,

Peter and his family, Reid and his family, and I assembled at the northwest end of the island to scatter Allan's ashes, as he had requested, so that he would always be in his favorite place.

Since that time, Reid and Margaret and Jason have spent all the time they possibly could at the island and have been most generous in sharing it with me.

Hopefully there will be many more generations of Wilsons to enjoy this wonderful, peaceful part of the earth.

The deaths of many other summer residents saddened us over these last two decades. Gladys Dickey, Gwen Erdmann, Ernie Pope, Leonard Giovannoli, Helen Grove, Jim Erdmann, Dudley Curry, Shirley McConnell—their names we add to the list of those who died earlier. We miss them all. We also miss those who have decided not to return. George and Sue Erdmann reluctantly made that decision in 1997 and there are others.

The story of our summers past here in Georgian Bay is one of many changes. There have been changes in the roster of cottagers, in the cottages themselves, and in our way of life. Recently we have begun to change the duration of our island season. In the first decades of our history cottagers began to arrive around July 1 and the last departed by September 1. Fortunate academics, as many of our original number were, might be in residence for both months. That pattern has changed and many cottagers come and go over a much longer season. Today one can expect to find cottages open and in use from Victoria Day in May through Canadian Thanksgiving in early October, although only Gary and Karin French can be expected to be in residence almost any weekend all year long! Unchanged, however, is the fact that we all still come to that day when the cottage must be closed and we must depart to await another season. Bob Donovan writes about, not endings, but pauses before another spring, another season:

I'm not sure I can speak of the summer of '82, though we were up in what was technically still summer, the last week in August and the first of September. The thermometer seemed to get stuck at 56 degrees during the day, whether you put it in the living room, on the porch, or in the water. At night, of course, it got much lower, once down to 46. That is the only island visit of my life when I didn't go swimming even once. Hope braved the icy water on most days, but she didn't dare take her favorite swim out to the shoal, since she was afraid I wouldn't go in after her if she got in trouble. Even so, we had a pleasant visit, since the Bakers, Erdmanns, Kochs, Malones, Franklins, and Hofmanns were all up, and we had a fairly busy social life. We had rarely been up so late in the season, and though the blueberries and most flowers were long gone, and even the songbirds had begun to depart, there was a certain austere beauty about the beginning of autumn that had its own charm. The maples and sumac had begun to turn, and flocks of blackbirds were beginning to migrate. The ospreys had raised their family and left, but we saw a bald eagle, a number of loons, many cormorants, and even a poor little hummingbird, looking desperately for flowers. Large flocks of young ducks began to assemble, preparatory to the big adventure of migration. We saw one flock of about thirty young mergansers (it's almost impossible to count them). Best of all, we were in the middle of French's Bay in a canoe when we heard a honking that presaged a flock of Canada geese, which we spotted almost directly overhead (much to the peril of our canoe). They came down near Fireplace Island, so we paddled over to see them in the water, but they took off in alarm as soon as they spotted us.

Faith and David came up in '83, David for the first time. He and Brian shared a passion for fishing and spent a good deal of their time at it, without, however, catching much of anything. Still, David remained cheerful. The fishing, he said, was good, it was just the catching that left something to be desired. The next year David could not get away, but Faith came up with a 9-month-old Caitlin, and Peter joined us for the first time in many years. Caitlin was not yet able to walk, but she zipped about the porch in her little wheel-mounted plastic chair. I'm sure it has a name of its own, but we called it the ankle-buster, for obvious reasons. Brian and Peter took an overnight canoe trip to the McCoys but met with disaster on their return, just at the mouth of Frederic Inlet, when Peter ill-advisedly stood up in the canoe to take a picture. Next day they were able to retrieve most of the things lost when the canoe overturned, including a cast iron skillet, and even some loose potatoes, which we later turned into a very good corned beef hash. Brian thought the recipe ought to begin, "soak six potatoes overnight in Georgian Bay...."

Brian brought Stas up in '87, the most recent member of our family to be introduced to Georgian Bay. They camped out in their well-designed tent most nights, but when the weather turned really nasty they could find refuge in the cottage, and of course they took their meals with the rest of us.

We verge on recent times, now, and as Seller and Yeatman put it, when you reach the present, history comes to a.

Like a sentence suddenly broken off, our history now comes to a pause. But only for a moment. In coming years others will be adding their stories of wonderful summers on the islands of Georgian Bay.

Epilogue

The story of our island community has not come to an end, of course, and one hopes that many more pages will be added to those found here. Some things, however, will probably always be the same. Certainly one would expect that what has meant so much to these cottagers over the years will continue to be as important to those still to come. First, Gary French reminds us of what we all have found to be true:

> The area is in my blood. For eighty years, Frenches have been going to French's Bay. The thought of watching Matthew grow up here, learning from fellow islanders the lore of this place, its people, its flora and fauna, exploring in his turn this wonderful paradise sends shivers up and down me. For these reasons, when people ask me where I live, I hesitate...because I "live" in the Bay and "work" in Toronto.

> I've always felt fortunate to have all my American friends. I have, however, found myself between two differing groups of

Americans at the cottage: the nature-loving, quiet, canoe paddling gentle people to the north and the partying, social friends
to the south in Frederic Inlet who come north from Ohio each
summer. Rod, Jane and Candy Cox, the Ludwigs, Stuckeys,
Spaethes and others, not forgetting the wonderful, kind and
humorous Canadians, Harrison and Florence Patte. The only
other Canadians I can think of are the Watsons (John, Denise,
and Andrew) on Nokomis, and, of course, the Wilsons, Rogers,
and McConnells. I have fond memories of Allan Wilson (who took
me flying and persuaded my parents to venture to the
Limestones aboard Tiki Too), of Reid Wilson who has delighted
us by his transformation from the captain of a boat called
Playboy, seldom seen running at less than full throttle, to avid
birdwatcher, botanist and canoeist. The words "Oogi-Oogi" bring
Pete McDonald to mind, while "Pictionary" summons up Linda
(ask her why the "girls" always lose!). And the Groves are needed to explain "PeaKnuckle." So many, John Stuckey, Bill
Spaethe, Dorothy Bergs, Nancy McDonald, Rod and Jane Cox,
Miss Hamilton, Florence and Harrison Patte, the senior
Erdmanns, Helen Grove and her kind husband, all have left their
impression on me and the collective impression I have that the
island, apart from the beauty and sanity it brings to my business
life today, is people. The island is what we share as our common
love and enjoy, each in his or her own way.

Gary has put into words the continuing importance all of us
find in the many people who have made, and will continue to make,
this a place we love. Babs Wilson speaks for us all to express the
value we place not only on sharing but also on solitude:

NOTHING BUT BEAUTY
Nothing But Peace

She awoke in the quiet grey of dawn in early July, and as she
looked at the peaked roof above her of the chalet type cottage
on their island, she heard the first sleepy chirping of the birds
outside.

It was so quiet here on Georgian Bay that the faintest sound
could be heard—the water breaking on the shoals at the outer

edge of the islands–the sweet plaintive song of the white-throated sparrow—the cry of a loon on its way to its favorite bay to dive for fish.

As the light grew brighter, she looked across the small bedroom to her husband, sleeping on a similar narrow bed to her own. He looked so peaceful that she hesitated to disturb him in order to have him share this moment with her. These were the times she loved the most, with the promise of a bright new day before her and the knowledge that there were two whole weeks that she could enjoy the serenity of this beautiful country. So she lay there for a few minutes, luxuriating in the comfort of her warm bed, and then she heard the crows starting their game of "let's wake up those lazy humans." Even their somewhat raucous cries had a significance. They sounded so much a part of life here in the peace and loveliness of nature unsullied by the sound of cars, trains and voices which abound in our large cities.

By now the sun was making its presence known. She sat up in bed and looked out of the window at the clear sky, the yellow, orange and red of the rising sun's rays making the blue look pale in comparison. She couldn't wait any longer. Leaving her husband asleep she quietly dressed and went down the wooden stairs to the cool living room below. The large windows looked out on the still water and the islands to the north. The smooth expanse of rock in front of the house was still damp from the dew, and the cobwebs on the cedar trees and bushes were plainly outlined by the water clinging to them. Now the birds were really greeting the new day, and she heard yellow warblers, song sparrows, myrtle warblers and many others that she could not identify, but all pouring out their joy of living on a summer day.

She slipped on a jacket, and opening the door, went out into the freshness of the early morning. She walked down to the water which was so still and clear that all the rocks around the shore were clearly defined. She felt she knew every rock that was there, as they were all old and familiar friends, and so she followed the shoreline towards the end of the island. As she passed some reeds and grasses there was a plop, and a small green frog sank to the bottom to hide in the silt. She sat down on a rock to wait for him to come to the surface, and then a movement towards the end of the island attracted her attention, and as she looked she saw a mink running over the rocks with its peculiar snake-like run. It stopped and looked in her direction—she did not move—and it continued on its way to the water where it dove for crayfish, and, catching one, proceeded to eat it there at the edge of the water. Then it smoothly became one with the water, and she could see its head forming an arrow as a ripple spread out on either side of it. It was the first movement to stir the glass-like surface, but, as if to a signal, at that moment she saw the first breeze caress that surface and felt the warmth of it on her face. By now the sun was well above the horizon; the day had begun. A boat started up in the distance and the hum of its motor came faintly to her, not disturbing the peace, but being a part of it, and she knew that some of her cottage neighbors couldn't resist this beautiful morning either. Now she was anxious to have her husband share this lovely day with her, so she walked slowly back to the cottage, wanting his company and yet reluctant to shatter this quiet moment that she had enjoyed alone.

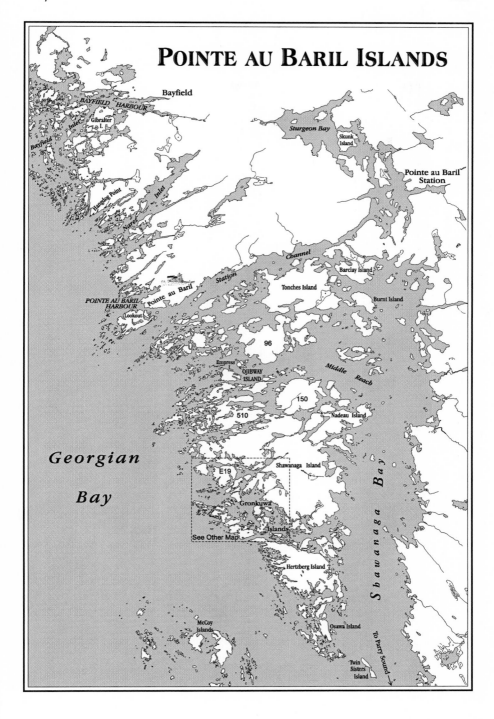

POINTE AU BARIL ISLANDS

Bayfield

BAYFIELD HARBOUR

Gibralter I.

Bayfield Inlet

Sturgeon Bay

Skunk Island

Pointe au Baril Station

Bangdog Point

Naret Inlet

Channel

Barclay Island

Tonches Island

Burnt Island

POINTE AU BARIL HARBOUR

Pointe au Baril Station

Lookout

96

Empress I.

OJIBWAY ISLAND

Middle Reach

150

510

Nadeau Island

Georgian

E19

Shawanaga Island

Bay

Gronkuwa

Islands

See Other Map

Hertzberg Island

Shawanaga Bay

McCoy Islands

Osawa Island

To Parry Sound

Twin Sisters Island

Group of Islands South of Carolyn

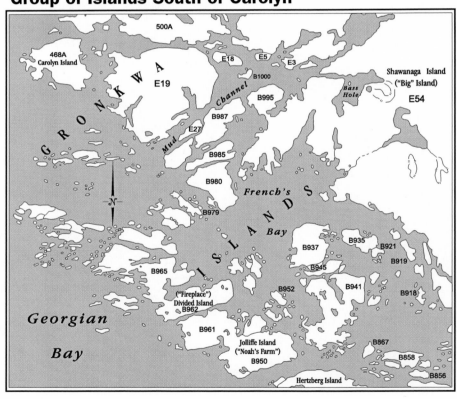

Gazeteer

There is an entry in the following gazeteer for each island whose cottagers figure in the history presented above. Not all islands owned and with cottages on them between Frederic Inlet and Carolyn are included here. Those whose islands lie south and east of a line drawn roughly from B 961 (Pine Island on our map) through B 941 (Leaming Island) to E 54 (Big Island) have not been included as historically their focus has been on Frederic Inlet rather than on French's Bay and Mud Channel as ours has been. Names of many (e.g. Charles Anderson, etc.) do appear from time to time in our stories, but they were not closely connected to our community. (Although this may be changing as powerboats shrink the distances between islands. Now Gary French looks south as well as north for ties to neighbors, for example.)

There are, thus, eighteen entries which follow. There is one island which is owned, B 962 (Fireplace or Divided Island), although its owners have never built a cottage on it and, while they may have camped from time to time, have remained unknown to our cottagers. It is thus included only for the sake of completeness.

For each of the eighteen the information provided is as complete as possible. Precise dates are given where known, but, where the approximate date seems not to be in question, I have not tried to check in Parry Sound to ascertain it more precisely. Dates for construction are very uncertain where additions or improvements are concerned. Where builders or contractors have been mentioned, they have been included as have prices. Finally, the names owners have given to their cottages or islands are listed when supplied. I have made every reasonable effort to insure that the information is accurate and complete, but this is not an official record and sometimes the information I have been given is contradictory. Still the names and dates which are important in our story may here be found in summary form.

B 918

SIZE: 1 Acre

OWNERS:

Lucy H. Young, 8/27/1915-11/20/1947	St. Louis, Missouri
Elsie B. Barber & Fanny Glad, 1947-9/23/1966	East Aurora, N.Y.
Elsie B. Barber, 1966-3/23/1973	East Aurora, N.Y.
Erwin J. & Elizabeth I. Freyberger, 1973—	Java, N.Y.
(Phillip B. & Kristine Spaeth Keller, tenants since 1980)	Hudson, Ohio

COTTAGE:
Built and occupied, 1916; fireplace built by Felix Laramie, 1923

NAMES:
Watahwaso; also known as "Lucy's Evening Star"

NOTE:
Sale price in 1947 was $1000

B 919

SIZE: 1.9 Acres

OWNERS:

Carrie Zahn Bartow, 9/1914-7/1969   Buffalo, N.Y.
—Chester, spouse; Chester, Jr.

Chester Bartow, Jr., 1969-1986   Buffalo, N.Y.

A. Dudley & Frances Y. Curry, 1986—   Edisto island, S.C.
—Eric Owen; Melissa M.

COTTAGES:
"Klondike Cottage" (16 x 10, plus 7 x 10 kitchen built by Olver Reid in 1915).
Bunk House built in 1979; house remodeled with porch in 1994.

NAME:
Inverurie

NOTE:
Original price in 1914 @ $10 per acre—$19, plus $20 for the survey.

B 921

SIZE: 8/10ths of an Acre

OWNERS:

James McBain Reid, 2/25/1925-4/28/1927   Pointe au Baril
—Margaret Estell Reid, spouse

Margaret Estell Reid, 1927-2/15/1960   Pointe au Baril
—James Olver Reid (son and administrator)

Leland A. & Itha W. Morton, 1960-9/15/1969   Port Orange, FL

A. Dudley & Francis Y. Curry, 1969-12/12/1977   Edisto Island, S.C.
—Eric Owen; Melissa Morrison
A. D., F.Y., E.O, & M.M. Curry, 1977—

COTTAGES:

Original built 1925; never occupied; demolished 1970. Current cottage built
1970 by Carman Emery. Bunk house built 1976 by owner

NAMES:

"Haunted House or Eagles Nest" before 1969; Petikuwa (Little Camp)

B 935

SIZE: 3.70 Acres

OWNERS:

Elizabeth Fuller, 10/16/1913-1937   Toronto, Ontario

Maggie (Peggy) Gatzka Hamilton, 1937-1975   Toronto, Ontario

John Hamilton Watson, 1975—   Willowdale, Ontario

—Denise, spouse; Andrew

COTTAGE:

Built in 1914; many additions over the years; indoor washroom,
toilet, 1970

NAME:

Nokomis (Ojibwa). A wise old woman who lived among the people—a
daughter of the moon; indeed she had once lived upon the moon with her
husband, but a jealous woman had pitched her into the middle of a lake and
she had fallen through to the earth—there she gave birth to a daughter,
Wenonah. From Tales of Nanabozho, by Dorothy M. Reid, Oxford University
Press.

NOTE: Miss Fuller received $800 for this property in 1937

B 9 3 7 North

SIZE: 13.88 Acres
(currently divided into two parcels—4.8 acres north and 9.1 acres south)

OWNERS:

Charles Garfield French, 10/31/1913-4/12/1943   Toronto, Ontario
—Mabel Louis, spouse; Steven C.

Steven C. French, 1943-8/28/1968   Toronto, Ontario
—Maggie, spouse; Sandra; John; Gary

Various owners, no occupants, 1968-10/4/1978

Rosemary Anne Phelan, 1978-12/6/1982   Toronto, Ontario

Elbert H. & Mary Ellen Baker (north parcel), 1982-   Hudson, Ohio
—Buff; Wendy; Martha; Nancy; Tim (see B 1000)

COTTAGES:

2 main cottages and 2 sleeping cottages built on the north parcel since 1982 (Frank Penfold, contractor for 3 and Stan Hodgson for the fourth)

NAMES:

Sagastaweekee (1913-1982); Wanong-Wabang

NOTE:

Property was purchased in 1913 for $163

B 937 South

SIZE:　13.88 Acres
(currently divided into two parcels—4.8 acres north and 9.1 acres south)

OWNERS:

Charles Garfield French, 10/31/1913-4/12/1943　　　　Toronto, Ontario
—Mabel Louis, spouse; Steven C.

Steven C. French, 1943-8/28/1968　　　　　　　　　Toronto, Ontario
—Maggie, spouse; Sandra; John; Gary

Various owners, no occupants, 1968-10/4/1978

Rosemary Anne Phelan, 1978-12/6/1982　　　　　　　Toronto, Ontario

Pete & Linda McDonald (south parcel), 1982-　　　　　Hudson, Ohio
—Marcie; Andy; Todd Sanders; Brad Sanders (Sharon, spouse)

COTTAGES:

One room (12 x 14) in 1919; many additions 1959-1968

NAMES:

Sagastaweekee (1913-1982); Timbers

NOTE:

Property was purchased in 1913 for $163

B 945

SIZE:　　1.6 Acres

OWNERS:

Florence Diehl, 12/26/1913-11/25/1920　　　　　　　　　Buffalo, N.Y.

Harry Giovannoli, 1920-2/13/1961　　　　　　　　　　　Lexington, KY
—Florence H. (Polly), spouse; Leonard; Robert

Florence H. & Leonard Giovannoli, 1961-1964　　　　　Lexington, KY

Steven C. French, 1964-8/13/1974　　　　　　　　　　Toronto, Ontario

Sandra French, 1974-1977　　　　　　　　　　　　　Toronto, Ontario

B. Garfield French (Gary), 1977—　　　　　　　　　Toronto, Ontario
—Karin, spouse; Matthew

COTTAGES:

"Klondike Cottage" built, 1913; additions (porches), 1920s; new guest cottage, 1985; new main cottage, 1994 (Frank Penfold, contractor)

NAMES:

Minne-ha-ha (1913-1920); Kenusa (1920-1964); Sagastaweekee

B 952

SIZE: 1.6 Acres

OWNERS:

Allan E. & Barbara Usher Wilson, 12/1959-1980   Toronto, Ontario
—Peter A. (Dorothy, spouse; Kevin; Darren); Reid J.

Reid J. & Margaret Weir Wilson, 1980—   Uxbridge, Ontario
—Jason M. R.

COTTAGE:

A-frame built by Allan and friends, 1960; addition (the Roost), 1990 (Neil West, builder)

NAME:

Shuh-Shuh-Gah (Blue Heron)

B · 9 6 2

SIZE: 20 Acres

OWNERS:

Marvin A. Ives, 12/8/1919-1923	San Francisco, CA
John R. Ives, 1923-1962	San Francisco, CA
John R. & Eileen B. Ives, 1962—	San Francisco, CA

COTTAGE:

None ever built; stone platform & fireplace only construction

NAME:

Known locally as Fireplace Island; on official maps Divided Island

B 979

SIZE: 1.8 Acres

OWNERS:

W. A. Tiffin, 1963-1981   Ottawa, Ontario

Karen Tiffin Hodgson, 1981-1990   Ottawa, Ontario

Tom McConnell, 1990—   Oakville, Ontario
—Shirley, spouse; Lisa; Nancy

COTTAGE:

Original, 1963; demolished, 1990. Three new cottages built, 1991 (Stan
Desmasdon, contractor); bunk house added, 1992

NAME:

The Hot Dog Stand

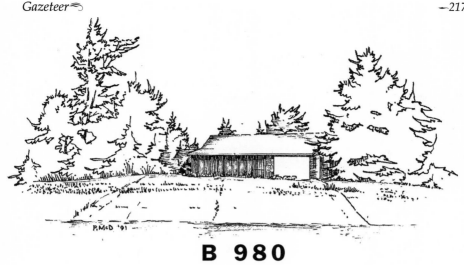

P.McD '91

B 980

SIZE: 17.5 Acres; parcel owned 5 acres

OWNERS:

John E. & Dorothy Dickey Donovan, 1933-1967   St. Louis, Missouri
—Dick (J.R.); Bob (R.A.); Bill (W.P.), Didge (D.G.); Betsy (M.E.)

Dorothy Dickey Donovan, 1967-1970   St. Louis, Missouri

John Richard Donovan, 1970—   St. Louis, Missouri
—Mildred, spouse; J. Michael (Donna, spouse; Tim; Scott; Kelly; Andrew;
Erin); Steven R. (see E 3); Susan Barbara

Robert Alan Donovan, 1970—   Guilderland, N.Y.
—Hope, spouse; Faith A. (David West, spouse; Caitlin); Peter A. (Erin, spouse;
Grace; Hugh); Brian R. (Stas, spouse; Larissa; Trevor; Ariadne)

William Patrick Donovan, 1970—   St. Paul, MN
—Patricia, spouse; Kevin P. (Molly, spouse; Sean; Bridget);
Maura G. (see E 27)

Dorothy Grace Donovan, 1970—   Downers Grove, IL

Mary Elizabeth Donovan, 1970—   St. Louis, Missouri

COTTAGES:

"Big House," 1934; addition, 1946; Bunk House, 1934; addition, 1969;
Apotheke, 1978 (C.Thorkildsen, J. & S. Hodgson, Frank Penfold).

NAME:

Eagle Island

B 985

SIZE: 5.5 Acres

OWNERS:

Helen Lewandowski Grove, 11/2/1931-5/1976   Basking Ridge, N.J.
—Clinton, spouse; Nancy; Judy; Clinton, Jr.

Nancy G. Malone, 1976—   Newton, N.J.
—Wendy (Steve Hofmann, spouse; Lonnie Ray); Steven; Jill; Margo (Mitch Friedman, spouse; Jessie; Carrie); Kevin (Haley Elijah); Chris

Judith G. Koch, 1976—   Ithaca, N.J.
—Heinz, spouse; Nanci (see B 987); Andrew (see B 987)

Clinton S. Grove, Jr., 1976—
—Heather

COTTAGES: Main cottage, 1931; porch added, 1934 (Thorkildsen, contractor); Bunk House, 1949 or 1950

NAME:

None given; known locally as Groves' Island

NOTE:

Purchase price in 1931, $140

B 987

SIZE:　　16 Acres

OWNERS:

Paul R. & Elfrieda Pope, 1919-1950　　　　　　　　　Ithaca, N.Y.
—Ernest; Elfrieda

Elfrieda Pope Bestelmeyer, 1950-1974　　　　　　　　Ithaca, N.Y.

Heinz & Judith G. Koch, 1974—　　　　　　　　　　　Ithaca, N.Y.
—Nanci (Drew Speer, spouse; Joshua; Samantha); Andrew (Beth, spouse;
Zachary

COTTAGES:

Original cottage, 1922-1923 (first occupied, 1924); addition, 1990.
Boat House, 1977 (Jack Thorkildsen, contractor). Guest cottage, 1997

NAME:

Fayola (name formed from two childhood imaginary kingdoms of Ernest
and Elfrieda Pope)

B 995

SIZE: 5.6 Acres

OWNERS:

Frederick C. Carter, 8/30/1913-4/18/1928   Toronto, Ontario

Walter Ellis Riley, 1928-8/7/1947   St. Louis, Missouri
—Robert A. Bergs (adopted son)

Robert A. Bergs, 1947—   Sarasota, FL
—Carol, spouse

COTTAGE:

Built, 1929; remodeled, 1955

NAME:

Belle Chasse (originally); known locally as Riley's Island, now Bergs'

NOTE:

Purchase price, 1913, $81

B 1000

SIZE: 0.5 Acres

OWNERS:

Ethel Williams (Plimpton), 1937-1949   Cleveland, Ohio

Elbert H. & Mary Ellen Baker, 1949—   Hudson, Ohio
—Buff (Tom Burkholder, spouse; Tolyn); Wendy (Kazunari Katakura, spouse; Kenji; Ichika; Seiji; Taisen); Nancy (Charlie Peters, spouse; Jim; Clara); Martha (Yosuke Tashiro, spouse; Hatsue; Ryo; Nobue; Shigeru); Tim (Hiroko, spouse; Jason Schock; Roger Schock; Alex; Sammy)

COTTAGE:

Originally a guest cottage, 1937; many additions.

NAMES:

Battleship, 1937-1949; Wabassin, 1949—

E 3

SIZE: 14.4 Acres, parcel owned approximately 2 acres

OWNERS:

Kate C. Whitelaw, 7/23/1936-8/26/1941	St. Louis, Missouri
Gladys Dickey, 1941-2/5/1957	St. Louis, Missouri
Gwendolyn Dickey Erdmann, 1957-2/7/1959 —Morris, spouse; James M.; George E.	Hammond, Indiana
James M. & George E. Erdmann, 1959-10/24/1969	Clermont, FL
George E. Erdmann, 1969-9/19/1979 —Susanne, spouse; Molly; Gwen; David	New York, N.Y.
Molly, Gwen, & David Erdmann, 1979-7/4/1986 (see E27)	Dallas, Texas
Steven R. & Sarah Donovan, 1986— —Julie (David Irwin, spouse); Katie	Denver, CO

COTTAGE:

Basic cottage, 1936; additions, 1937-1941 (Thorkildsen); Wash House, 2000 (Penfold)

Name: None given; known locally as E 3

E 5

SIZE: 1.2 Acres

OWNERS:

Helen Whitelaw & Gladys Dickey, 1922-1941   St. Louis, Missouri

Helen Whitelaw, 1941-1953   St. Louis, Missouri

Ralph & Dorothy Foutz, 1953-1966   Tiffin, Ohio
—Molly (Mary); Tiny (Helen); Jean

David & Jean Foutz Hofmann, 1966—   Edwardsville, IL
—Steven C. (see B 985); Lisa G. (Beaumont); Lora L. (Benedetti); Kurt J.;
Karla J. (Sheeley)

COTTAGE:

Built, 1924; first occupied, 1926. Fireplace, porches, kitchen, by 1930
(Thorkildsen); Porch enclosed, 1999; Bunk House, 2000 (Stan Hodgson)

NAMES:

Known locally simply as E 5 until 1953; Currently, Kingbird

NOTE:

Sale price in 1953, $850

E 18

SIZE: 3.8 Acres

OWNERS:

Ethel M. Williams, 12/3/1930-6/11/1948   Cleveland, Ohio
—Sam Plimpton, spouse

Ralph & Dorothy Foutz, 1948-11/30/1966   Tiffin, Ohio
—Molly (Mary); Tiny (Helen); Jean

Jim & Molly I. Franklin, 1966—   Kingston, N.Y.
—Linda Sue; John Michael (Jane, spouse; Danny; Margaret; Katie); James
William (Patty, spouse; Brian; Scott; Kyle); Eve Ellen

COTTAGE:

Main cottage built, 1931 (on McDonald's plan); Bunk House, 1937

NAME:

Chinook

E27

SIZE: 　2.3 Acres

OWNERS:

D. Reuben & Eleanor K. Read, 12/10/1932-1945 　　　　　 Elsah, IL
—Betsy (Elizabeth)

Eleanor K. Read, 12/11/1945-7/31/1957 　　　　　　　　 Elsah, IL
—Betsy (Holt)

George E. & Susanne Erdmann, 1957-1998 　　　　 Palm City, FL
—Molly (Ivan Shomer, spouse; Matthew, Paul); Gwen; David
(Tiffany, Susie)

David A. Whitman & Maura G. Donovan, 1998— 　　　 St. Paul, MN
—Alexander; Peter

COTTAGES:

Built, 1933 & demolished, 1957. New cottage, 1957; porch, 1958; boat house,
1964; bunk house, 1987 (new cottage a prefab; all other construction by
George Erdmann)

NAMES:

Peace (1932-1956); "The Island" (1957-1997); Shingebiss, 1998—

Notes

Notes

Notes